ABUNDANCE

Also by Faith Winters

Trauma Healing Series - Book 4

ABUNDANCE

Create Confidence,
Contentment and Happiness

Faith Winters

www.FaithfulHabits.com

Trauma Healing Series - Book 4

ABUNDANCE: Create Confidence, Contentment and Happiness

Author: Faith Winters

First Printing: August 2021

Paperback ISBN: 978-1-7377164-64

Library of Congress Control Number:

Faithful Habits Press

www.faithfulhabits.com

Editor: Rochelle Dean

Contact the author at: Author@faithfulhabits.com

To order bulk copies for groups contact: Info@faithfulhabits.com

About the author

Faith Winters is a mental health professional with nearly two decades of experience. She is an expert who has taught thousands of people how to live calmer, more fulfilling lives. She is an author of books focused on helping people to heal and grow. Faith has mentored and trained many other mental health professionals.

Trauma Healing Series Outline

Trauma Healing Series.com

Trauma Healing Series

The Trauma Healing series explores the challenges of a life affected by bullying, trauma, abuse, neglect, domestic violence, substance use, and chaos. This series compares the differences between a trauma-affected life and a healthy functional life. The series is designed to help those impacted by trauma to process their past in a healing way. Lowering the barriers that hinder growth and moving forward toward understanding, healthy functioning, and a life of abundance.

A trauma is any disturbing experience that results in significant fear, helplessness, dissociation, confusion, or other disruptive feelings intense enough to have a long-lasting negative effect on a person's attitudes, behavior, and other aspects of functioning. Traumatic events may challenge a person's view of the world as a reasonable, safe, and predictable place.

Processing the past is the act of making sense of an experience, putting it to rest, and can include achieving the resolution needed to move on from a traumatic experience. If some aspect of trauma is not processed, it may continue to cause problems in the present until it can be put to rest.

Many individuals experience trauma during their lifetimes. Although some people exposed to traumatic events demonstrate few lingering symptoms, other people, especially those who have experienced repeated, chronic, or multiple traumas are more likely to have many struggles and after-effects, including emotional distress, substance abuse, physical and mental health problems.

Many individuals who seek help and recovery have histories of trauma. But they often do not recognize the impact past trauma has had on their lives. Either they do not draw connections between their past trauma and their current struggles. Or they may try to avoid thinking about hard times altogether. Time alone does not heal most trauma; healthy processing is a vital part of the healing dynamic.

Trauma Healing Series

Trauma Healing Series explores the differences between a healthy, functional life and a wounded life impacted by the lingering effects of bullying, abuse, trauma, neglect, domestic violence, substance use, and chaos. The series is designed to help lower the barriers that hinder growth and healing so you can move forward toward the freedom of thriving.

Trauma Healing Series - Book 1

FUNDAMENTALS

Escape the Lingering Effects of Bullying, Abuse, or Trauma

By learning your fundamental rights, developing inner awareness of your strengths, and understanding the contrast to past chaos you will step into freedom and abundance, security, and significance, and be happy. Explore how to have more peace within yourself, better relationships with others, more freedom and contentment, no matter what is going on around you.

Trauma Healing Series - Book 2

RESTORATION

Living as Designed in Joy and Peace

You are designed to have joy, peace and be able to heal from the wounds of life. Look deeply into your unique design. Put to rest the old wounds that trap you into painful patterns of responding to life and hinder your healing. By exploring healthy patterns of living you can be living your best life after trauma. You can have restoration.

Trauma Healing Series - Book 3

CONNECTIONS

Master the Art of Relationship

When you do what it takes to develop wholesome social habits and essential boundary skills, you can have good relationships now and in the future, no matter what your past relationships were like. By learning key skills for a healthy lifestyle and safe, healthy relationships you will unlock the power of community to discover your significant place in the world.

Trauma Healing Series - Book 4

ABUNDANCE

Create Confidence, Contentment and Happiness

You can have the confident freedom of contentment, recognizing and enjoying the abundance of life around you. Contentment is not the fulfillment of what you want, but the realization of what you already have. By using the principles in this book, you will derive a richness of life that goes far beyond the temporary rewards of success and create lasting happiness for yourself in any situation.

Table of Contents

PART THREE : Abundance - Components of a Happy Life

WHAT THIS BOOK IS ABOUT

Even though life has difficulties, we can live in abundance, having confidence, contentment, and happiness. Abundance refers to having more than an adequate supply, to have plenty or more than you need. Abundance is the opposite of scarcity.

Abundance was written to help people find the confidence, contentment, and happiness of responsible adulthood. Learning these skills will bring joy and happiness. Within these pages, we explore the freedoms and joys of responsible adulthood. We will look at the skills adults use and the powers they have, as well as how adults live an abundant life by cultivating confidence, learning contentment, and creating happiness for themselves and others. You can have this freedom too, recognizing and enjoying the richness of life around you, whether you have little or much. You can leave behind the crippling mindset of scarcity and its struggles, developing the mature habits of an abundance mentality, healthy relationships, a heart at peace, and diligent choices that move toward looking at your future with confidence.

As the fourth book in the Trauma Healing Series, *Abundance* will look in-depth at the primary principles on which a healthy adult life is based, the way we are designed to function. The other three books in the series: *Fundamentals*, *Restoration*, and *Connections*, explore the foundational principles of healing from trauma and go deeply into the skill-building process of healing old wounds and moving into a pattern of healthy living.

ABOUT FAITH'S QUALIFICATIONS

As a child, I grew up in an abusive home, having experienced bullying, abuse, trauma, trouble, chaos, and the resulting problems that hinder healthy, mature development in a number of areas of life. The childhood wounds to our hearts and self-worth do not often heal on their own. They need some intentional help to heal. I learned ways to cope with the wounds. While those coping techniques allowed me to survive as a child, those same learned habits crippled areas of my life as an adult and made each day harder than it needed to be.

We need to know how to live the type of healthy life that removes barriers to healing. Through a healing process, I learned how to value myself, have boundaries with others, and find the freedom of wise decision-making. Now I live a confident, contented, happy life with a calling to help others to escape the pains of the past.

God has brought me into an abundant life, and I want to help others to heal and to grow. I want there to be less pain in the world. My journey has uniquely qualified me to help others toward a healthier life.

- **Experience in living for decades with struggles** – I grew up in traumatic circumstances and spent decades as an adult dealing with anxiety, panic attacks, and PTSD Post Traumatic Stress Disorder. In the midst of those painful years, I learned valuable lessons in surviving struggles, and the need for healing.

- **Healing process** – I went through psychoeducational classes, extensive reading, and professional mental health therapy. As my anxiety ended, the panic attacks ceased, and the PTSD was finally gone, I wanted to help others to escape the traumas of the past and to heal and grow.

- **Education** – I then decided to attend university to get a master's degree in counseling so I would have the professional therapeutic skills to help others heal from trauma in effective ways.

- **Experience in teaching these key skills to others** – For more than a decade, I have worked as a professional counselor and have taught thousands of people how to deal with struggles, heal from trauma, and live calmer, healthier, happier lives even in the midst of struggles.

In this book, we will explore the healthy design of responsible adulthood and how it brings us into an abundant life of freedom and contentment. If you address the emotional, physical, and intellectual principles presented in this book, you can have a healthier life. By living the principles of a healthy lifestyle, you can live unhindered by the debilitating effects of past traumas and experience abundance.

My promise to you, dear reader, is that as you read the principles presented in this book, you will have before you many of the concepts needed for a healthier, happier life. If you implement two or three of the principles found in these pages, you will find that you will experience a happier, more contented life. It will take some effort on your part, but the skills you need to develop to move forward are here in your hands. If you apply five or six of these principles, it can literally change the course of your life and have a positive effect on people around you. If you apply all the ideas in this book, you will discover a revolution inside, a return to something even more powerful than happiness. That is the presence of peace.

Throughout this four part Trauma Healing series, we have based a lot of the principles we discuss on our basic rights as human beings. In the first book Fundamentals, we explored that deeply. In Abundance, we go forward to look at how these are lived out.

Your Rights as a Human Being

In this section, I have organized our rights into the broad categories of individual rights, relationship rights, and freedom rights. In the three parts of this book, I discuss each of these rights in detail and help you build a foundation for healing from your trauma. Understanding each of these rights and living from a place that respects these rights in yourself and in others is an important key that unlocks healing from trauma and freedom from lingering effects of past bullying, abuse, trauma, trouble, or chaos.

Individual rights include how we interact with ourselves, the boundaries we set up, and understanding what is our own and what is not ours. Individual rights include the basic ways we can expect to be treated and the basic ways we treat others, with dignity and respect.

- You have the right to be you and to love and be loved.
- You have the right to make mistakes, to be human – not perfect.
- You have the right to say NO.
- You have the right to choose your own values and beliefs.
- You have the right to your own feelings and opinions and to express them.
- You have the right to change your mind and your life.

Relational rights are the rights that we have as we relate to other people: family, friends, bosses, children, parents, neighbors, a significant other, and all the different people that we interact with in life. Relational rights provide healthy ways to interact with people.

- You have the right to be safe, to be treated with dignity and respect.
- You have the right to healthy friendships.
- You have the right to choose when and how your body is touched.
- You have the right to treat yourself as well as you treat others.
- You have the right not to be responsible for other adults' choices, feelings, and behavior.
- You have the right to feel angry and leave if you are treated abusively.

Freedom rights are the freedoms that we have individually and collectively to make our own choices of what we want to do and how we want to move forward in our life. These are the responsibilities and choices we have as adults.

- You have the right to your own privacy, personal space, and time.
- You have the right to make your own decisions about your life.
- You have the right to ask questions about anything that affects your life.
- You have the right to request what you want.
- You have the right to earn and control your own resources.
- You have the right to not be liked by everyone.

When we consider our rights as a human, some questions come up:

- How do we know we have these rights?
- Where do they come from?
- What does the word rights even mean?

Dictionaries define rights as the basic rules about what people are allowed or owed, being in accordance with what is just, good, or proper. Human Rights are the basic rights and freedoms that belong to every person in the world, from birth until death.

Another authority about rights is the Declaration of Independence of the United States of America. That document tells us these rights were highlighted as the rights of the people when our nation was formed.

We hold these truths to be self-evident, that all men are created equal, that they are endowed by their Creator with certain unalienable Rights, that among these are Life, Liberty, and the pursuit of Happiness.

Further rights are discussed in the other founding documents of the USA, the Constitution, and the Bill of Rights.

Yet another place where rights are defined is in the document of the United Nations "The Universal Declaration of Human Rights."

"Whereas recognition of the inherent dignity and of the equal and inalienable rights of all members of the human family is the foundation of freedom, justice, and peace in the world,"

This author sees all these basic rights as principles that come out of the scriptures. These are the rights

God describes and models for us throughout the Bible.

What we understand from all these authoritative writings is that:

As humans we have fundamental rights.

Limitations to our rights

Since ALL humans have fundamental rights, our rights and freedoms may end where another person's rights begin. Also, there may be times in life where, through our own choices or the choices of others, we may not have full access to all of these rights for a period of time.

Examples:

- When someone chooses to go into a treatment program or a recovery community.
- When someone chooses to live in a situation with others where these rights are not respected or regarded.
- Through no choice of our own, we are in a situation where these rights are not available to us.

That does not mean our rights do not exist, it means that for a while they are not fully available to us.

One of the examples is when someone chooses to go to a recovery community to get help because they are trying to recover from addiction, homelessness, trauma, etc. They have found a community that is willing to help them, perhaps without cost. But it is not a free hotel. The community is willing to help, providing a place to sleep, food to eat, and the other components of life; but there is still an exchange. So, when someone chooses to come into the community, they are also choosing to follow the program of those who run the community. So, for a period of time, they are choosing to limit some of their own freedoms and rights so that they can receive the benefits that the community offers. For example, in a recovery community, your choice of what to eat when may be limited to what the community offers. Your use of your time may be shaped by the schedule that the community dictates.

Learn about your rights

It is never too late. Anyone can learn about their fundamental rights as a human and begin to change their lives to live to respect those rights for themselves and to respect those rights for all those around them. It starts with learning about the fundamental rights of an individual.

PART ONE

Having Confidence

When you have confidence, it gives a sense of power and freedom to your life. Having confidence is the feeling or belief that you can do something well; a calm reliance on yourself, someone else, or something. Self-confidence is a skill you can build and strengthen. It is the authority of responsible adulthood and knowing when you are doing the right things at the right times, in the right ways for the right reasons. Confidence is a learned skill that anybody can acquire. It takes some effort, but there are building blocks to confidence available to you.

CHAPTER 1

What Confidence Looks Like

Confidence is an inner strength that is displayed through outer habits. When we have spent the time and effort to know ourselves and our skills, we develop a calm confidence that makes life easier and more effective. Confidence does not need to be aggressive, but rather it is firm and decisive.

Description of a Person with Confidence

A person with confidence is generally very easy to be around. They are at ease in most situations. They have a sense of direction and self-assurance. They show that they have a strong core value by the respectful way they treat others and expect to be treated themselves. Since they feel at ease within themselves, the people they are around can feel at ease as well.

They do not burden others with the details of their rough day, or the frustrations they have experienced. They relate information, even negative information, in ways that are respectful and neutral. A confident person gains people's trust easily but does not demand it.

A person with confidence has a healthy sense of self-worth and a realistic acceptance of their own strengths and weaknesses. They have poise, self-assurance, and self-awareness, as well as a positive outlook and a habit of growing.

The Layers of Displaying Confidence

When we notice a confident person, a lot of different aspects add up to us trusting them. That includes physical stance, posture, and the way they move in the world. Their eye contact is steady, respectful, and honest. They are respectful of personal space.

It is important for us to look at all these details because if we have spent years with low confidence, it is likely we have developed the displayed habits of low confidence. When we want to move into a more confident way, we may need to examine our habits and shift them toward the confidence that we feel now, not the attitudes of the past. Let's look at some of these aspects of displayed confidence in more depth.

Posture Habits of a Person with Confidence

Confident people generally stand and sit up straight. Their posture is a comfortable attentiveness: feet aligned with shoulders; weight evenly distributed. They turn their body toward the person they are listening to. A way to visualize this posture is to imagine a string pulling your head and spine toward the ceiling. This elongates your neck, improves your posture and stature, allows your lungs more space to breathe deeply helping you look and feel more confident. Try it right now and see what your feel.

Eye Contact Habits of a Person with Confidence

Confident behavior includes appropriate eye contact. What constitutes appropriate eye contact can vary in different cultures. In my culture, looking someone in the eyes is a part of open, friendly, honest, and confident behavior. Staring for too long could be seen as intimate, aggressive, or threatening, and could make others feel uncomfortable. Avoiding looking someone in the eyes could be perceived as closed off, dishonest, untrustworthy, or sneaky. Confident eye contact in my culture is to look someone in the eyes, glance away every moment or two, then look back. Glancing away for a second or two lowers the intensity, and continuing to look back holds an honest and open gaze without signaling intimacy, pressure, or aggression.

Your tasks here include examining your own personal comfort with eye contact. Observe how you feel when speaking with different people who use different eye contact habits. Observe your own habits of eye contact when you feel confident and when you feel uneasy. Once you have noticed these habits, you can move your own eye contact habits toward the habits of a confident person.

Personal Space Habits of a Confident Person

Confident people are aware of and respect the personal space needs different situations call for. They can decide on the right personal space to give according to culture, situation, and the individuals they are with and then respect those boundaries.

Your first task here is to understand your own need for personal space and how that varies from situation to situation. In my culture, the confident, comfortable space we need to feel both separate and connected to others varies from person to person and from situation to situation. For family members we feel confident with and close to, comfortable space can be quite close, perhaps only a hand width apart, and touch might be welcomed. For strangers waiting at an open bus stop or in a large lobby waiting for an elevator, a comfortable space may be far enough apart that even if both people reach out their arms, they would still not be touching. However, once onboard a crowded bus or elevator, the comfortable space may be quite close, but still being careful not to brush onto others who are less than a hand width away.

Once you have assessed your own confident and comfortable space, look at the others you are around and notice what each of them sees as a comfortable space. Having confidence is about treating others with dignity and respect, which includes paying attention to the amount of personal space they seem to be comfortable with and honoring their boundaries.

Self-Confidence

A confident person has a sense of control in their life. They have a realistic understanding of their strengths and weakness and still have a positive view of themselves. They set realistic expectations and goals for them themselves and others, they communicate assertively, and they can handle criticism with humility and grace. Self-confidence is an attitude you have about your own skills and abilities.

People with a healthy sense of self-confidence are able to feel good about themselves and know that they deserve respect from others. A self-confident person believes they can do things well, without having an attitude of arrogance.

Self-Doubt

When you feel inferior, full of self-doubt, you may have difficulty trusting others. You may feel unworthy, unloved, or be sensitive to criticism. Your attitude may be passive or submissive. When you doubt yourself, you can spend more time wondering what other people are thinking of you than you spend focusing on developing your own competence.

Confidence Is Not Arrogance

Additionally, the need to show off and brag to feel confident often comes from insecurity. Ridiculing others and putting others down can come from a core a lack of self-confidence, even if it comes off as arrogance. A confident person does not need to push others down to build themselves up. They can quietly build up their own confidence by gaining strength, knowledge, and skills. True confidence often appears somewhere in the middle of the two extremes of insecurity and arrogance, both of which are symptoms of a lack of true self-confidence.

> *"You gain strength, courage and confidence*
> *by every experience in which you really*
> *stop to look fear in the face.*
> *You are able to say to yourself,*
> *'I have lived through this horror.*
> *I can take the next thing that comes along.'*
> *You must do the thing you think you cannot do."*
> *— Eleanor Roosevelt,*

Ways to Increase Confidence

- Remember that your past does not define you. Today is the day you are strengthening your new reputation.
- Recognize what you do well: the strengths you have, the skills you have, and your positive character traits.
- Recognize that other people are not responsible for your feelings. You can deal with your own emotional issues; you can make the changes to improve your life.
- Acknowledge mistakes. You have the right to make mistakes. Mistakes help us to grow and learn.

- Surround yourself with people who love and respect you for who you are.
- Continue to learn new skills and build your knowledge. Make it a habit to learn more about your field and other fields of study.
- Break large tasks or goals into smaller steps and then recognize each step you accomplish. Take a few moments to enjoy the accomplishment.
- Remember you have the right to say 'No.'
- Take time to think through your available choices and the many different ways to reach a goal.
- Once you have considered and chosen the best course of action, stop deciding and just move forward. The hardest part of a task can be starting. Don't put it off, start now.
- Communicate your needs, wants, feelings, and opinions directly with respect for others' needs, wants, feelings, and opinions.
- Understand that life is always going to be messy. The sooner you accept this, the more you are able to confidently focus on the good rather than the bad.
- Life will always have new challenges, but your attitude about these challenges can strengthen or weaken your confidence.

Professional Help

Working with a mental health therapist can help you target specific areas for healing and growth to develop a stronger self-confidence. You can grow in your confidence and in your courage. You are not stuck with the amount you had yesterday. As you exercise these skills, they grow stronger. Confidence has the authority of responsible adulthood and knowing when you are doing the right things at the right times, in the right ways for the right reasons.

In Summary

Confidence is an inner quality of a solid core. When you have confidence it gives a sense of power and freedom to your life. Having confidence is the feeling or belief that you can do something well. Confidence is a learned skill that makes life easier and more effective. Self-confidence is a skill you can build and strengthen. Confidence shows up in every aspect of a person's life, from how they carry themselves to how they interact with others.

CHAPTER 2

Confident Freedom of Adulthood

Adults have tremendous freedom. We get to choose to do what we want when we want. We get to choose what to do with our time and how to spend our money. We don't have to ask permission to believe a certain way or think a certain way. We get to choose what is important to us.

Children live under the authority of others. They need the help and the direction of others to know how to interact in life. Becoming a confident adult involves being able to make your own decisions, take on your own responsibilities, and to be able to interact with others on an equal basis. Children and adolescents interact with adults on a one-up or one-down basis. Adults interact with other adults on a basis of equality. However, one's chronological age is not the only factor in how they interact with the world. It's possible to get stuck in childhood or adolescence in our emotions, in how we relate to others, or in our decision-making processes. We may need the help of a professional counselor to learn how to break free of childish cycles or adolescent thinking patterns and experience the confidence of adulthood.

As adults, we do not have to ask permission or put up with people telling us exactly what we can and cannot do. However, even in adulthood, people can get stuck in pre-adult ways of thinking. To them, everything looks black and white. They can also get stuck in judging other people for not doing something like they are doing it. They look down on everybody else, not respecting the diversity we are created with.

The Freedom of Childhood

There are times I've heard people say, '*I wish I had the freedom I had when I was a kid. Those were carefree days.*' Would you really want to return to carefree childhood? As children, we had limited freedom. Sure, the responsibilities were small. But so were the freedoms. Other people made your choices for you: where you could go, what you could do, what to wear, even what to eat. People can get stuck in childish patterns of interacting in the world. We begin to grow out of that when we accept responsibility for our actions and choices.

Getting Stuck on Fairness

I want life to be fair, but the reality is that life is not fair. Especially for me. Think about it: if you have two and I have one, I might think well, that's not fair and get indignant about it. And yet, when I have two and you have one, I don't seem to care as much about fairness. This is what it's like to get stuck in childhood. I may state that I am focused on fairness, but it may seem that it is only as far as I think things should be fair for me.

But do I want what I've got coming to me? Think about that statement again. Do you really want what you've got coming to you? Have you ever made wrong choices? Have you ever done anything that caused stress or trouble for others? Do you want the consequences of every bad choice you have ever made in your life? I don't. What I want is mercy. I know that I have not made all the choices in my life well and I want mercy. Knowing that mercy is so important, I'm going to give mercy to others. Fairness is not enough. I do not want just fairness; I want to love mercy enough to share mercy and give mercy. If I am passionate about fairness, I can choose to make life's choices more fair for all those around me.

Getting Stuck in Adolescence

Adolescents are trying hard to figure out what it takes to be an adult, and yet they're also stuck in the immaturity of black-and-white or immature thinking. Part of the passage into adulthood is figuring out what's mine and what my own values are, not just accepting the values of the adults around me. Adolescents are seeking to understand and choose their own values. It is a time to figure out where they need to ask permission and where they have the freedom to figure that out for themselves. Becoming a confident adult is easier when we have taken time to struggle through and resolve these kinds of adolescent issues.

However, people who have experienced trauma can get the stuck feeling they need permission because their emotions can get stuck in an adolescent place. They haven't yet completed that forward movement into the confident freedom of adulthood. Therefore they have more need for the approval of others. All of us like to have the approval of others at times. But when that becomes a huge emotional need, it is likely we are still stuck in adolescent emotions. Moving forward is learning how to access your own actions and give yourself the appropriate affirmations based on your objective assessment.

Maturity toward the freedom of adulthood includes developing the ability to feel uncomfortable emotions and be in difficult situations without needing someone else to bail you out or fix it for you. You have the freedom to make your own choices, but also the freedom to work through your own difficulties. As you problem solve more and more often, your confidence grows.

The Need for Permission

There are times and places in life that we have the authority to decide to do or not to do something and we don't need to ask anybody else's permission. However, there are other times and places in life where we need to ask for permission because we don't have the authority to do something. This is true when we are children when we need to ask permission for most things. But it remains true in some situations as adults.

In Summary

Adults have tremendous freedom to choose what to do with our time, how to spend our money, what to think, what friends to have, and what is important. Sometimes people can get stuck in childish or adolescent patterns of interacting in the world. We grow out of that when we understand that life is not always fair, and we accept responsibility for our actions and choices. You have the freedom to make your own choices, but also the freedom to work through your own difficulties. As you work to problem solve your own difficulties more and more often, your confident freedom adulthood grows.

CHAPTER 3

Confident Authority of Adulthood

Adults don't need permission from other people for what to think, or feel, or how they can act. Adults make their own decisions. They have their own opinions. They establish their own values. Adults are not subject to the approval of others for everything they do. Adults are responsible for their own behavior and for any consequences for their behaviors. There is tremendous freedom in becoming an adult—and also a tremendous responsibility.

As adults, we have the authority to choose where we go, what we do, what our activities are, and who our friends are. In our personal lives, we have the authority to make all our own choices. When we live in a family, community, and nation, we may take into consideration how our choices may affect others out of a sense of kindness and generosity. But we have the authority to choose what job we want to apply for, where we want to live, and what kind of vehicle we want to have or not have. This authority gives us the freedoms that we have as an adult, and with those freedoms come responsibilities.

Confident adults exercise authority in their personal lives because they understand what is under their control and what is not. They have developed the maturity, skills, and expertise to care for their own lives and the lives of those who depend on them.

Example in Choice of Work

In their work, confident adults exercise the authority over their area of expertise because they have the education, skill, training, and experience that is needed for a specific task or purpose. Adults also take direction from those who have education, skill and training for a particular purpose and adults can follow these directions go forward.

If there is a job we want, we first need to be qualified for the job with our education and our experience, which means we might have to take jobs we'd rather not have simply because we need to get the experience in order to work toward the job we really want.

In order to live where we want and do the kind of work we really want to do; we may have to make some long-term plans. Since we have the authority to choose what we want, we can choose to take a close look and decide what we really want. Then we examine what is between us and where we want to be. We may need to increase our skills and experience, get more education, or build a wider social network.

I know where I want to be, what I want to do. But it seems out of reach. Is it really? Perhaps this is a good time to re-assess your goal. Is it viable? If your goal is to be a racehorse jockey and your body has a large bone structure and you are very tall, that goal may be out of reach, and you need to reassess. If you want to be an astronaut and your eyesight is poor, that may not work out. If you want a job that requires a master's degree and you have only high school education, that is still a viable goal, it will just take some extra planning and time as you work toward the education required.

The Reality of NOW

When we have decided what we really want to do and looked at what is between us and the goal, we can come face to face with the reality of NOW. We need to be able to keep a roof over our head and be able to buy food now. The goal is what I want, but I need to feed myself and my family this week. In that case, you may need to take an available job to pay the bills while you plan and work at getting the education, skills, and training for the work you really want. There are many resources around to help you. Having a plan and working diligently toward it, you will become aware of more of the resources. Your greatest resource is access to your Creator and the strengths he has placed within you. You have more opportunities than you will ever be able to use and more diligence and creativity than you know. However, sometimes we are afraid to move forward for fear of making a mistake.

Making Mistakes

A key aspect to being an adult is the ability to accept correction. All of us make mistakes; mistakes are not the biggest problem. It is what you do after you make the mistake that can be a problem or not. When we find we have made a mistake, do we reach out to correct that mistake? The problem multiplies when we try to sneak and deny that we did it, or blame it on somebody else. Exercising the authority of confident adulthood includes being able to admit your own mistakes and deal with the consequences, then learn from what went wrong and move forward.

Exercising the confident authority of responsible adulthood is something we learn over time, especially since not all of us were raised in nurturing homes where we saw a responsible adult handling life well. What happened to us as children is not our fault, but the kind of adult you become is totally under your authority and is your responsibility. Your attitudes and your values are your responsibility because you get to choose those.

Submitting to Authority

Confident adults not only exercise authority, but they also submit to authority. Among the first things that we learn as children is that we are not in charge of everything. There are people telling us what to do.

We were taught to obey parents, teachers, and other adults who would tell us what to do, where to go, and how to behave. These were the same people who provided the food, clothing, shelter, and other resources we needed to survive. Often, there would be negative consequences if we did not obey, so our obedience was required or even forced. However, as we matured, obedience became something we could choose to do or not; we might choose to deal with the consequences instead. Making those choices is a part of the journey to adulthood.

Being able to choose obedience and submitting to authorities is an important aspect of adult life. Obedience is an important aspect of freedom. It changes from something required of us to something we choose to do. When we drive a vehicle, we submit to the laws concerning driving. We have to study those laws in order to get our driver's license. We rely on other drivers generally submitting to those same laws. That way the vehicles stay on their own section of the roadway and appropriate stops and intersections are made. Submitting to the authority about driving makes traveling safer for everyone.

Some people struggle with submitting to authority. They are constantly in that adolescent mindset of trying to figure out where their power and expertise are. They think that if they tear down an authority, it will make them strong and confident. It doesn't. What that makes them is rebellious. A confident adult can work diligently to change things that need to be changed about authority, but they do it while thinking how their choices will affect all those concerned, not just their own interests.

> *He has shown you, O mortal, what is good.*
> *And what does the Lord require of you?*
> *To act justly and to love mercy and*
> *to walk humbly with your God.*
> Micah 6:8

Let's explore this passage and what it means for a confident adulthood. To do justice means that I'm doing the next right thing. However, just because I'm doing what I believe is right doesn't mean I'm demanding everybody else do things the way I do things. It means that I'm thinking carefully about how I can do things right. To love mercy means to give grace to other people when they don't do things like I do or when they make mistakes, knowing that I make mistakes all the time. I'm going to interact with others knowing that I need mercy, too. To walk humbly before my God means knowing that he has seen every mistake I have ever made in my life and yet he still loves me. He knows every mistake I will make in the future and yet he still loves me. He is God, and I am not, and I am grateful for his love and his care. I can have confidence in his love as I continuously learn how to act justly in my daily life, as I seek to give grace, and as I recognize his position as Lord and mine as human.

In Summary

God has given us the authority as adults to have command over our own lives. We make our own choices, and we don't rely on others to tell us what to do. Adults have the authority to make their own decisions, have their own opinions, and establish their own values. Adults are not subject to the approval of others for everything they do. This authority gives freedom and with that freedom comes responsibility. Confident adults exercise authority over their area of expertise because they have the maturity, skill, and experience that is needed. Exercising the authority of confident adulthood includes being able to admit your own mistakes and deal with the consequences. Confident adults not only exercise authority, but they also submit to authority.

CHAPTER 4

Skills and Confidence

When we have skills and competence, it is easy to feel confident. Competence is developed as our talents and strengths are recognized and built up. We have a sense that we are good at trying. Even when life gets stressful, we figure out how to cope. We work through difficult problems and mistakes, expanding our knowledge and skill along the way; our accomplishments are the result of a combination of ability, effort, study, training, practice, and experience. When we have competence, we have the skills and ability to do something successfully.

Confidence is preparation.
Everything else is out of your control.
Richard Kline

The Ability to Do Something Effectively

Competence is the set of characteristics, attitudes, and skills that demonstrate and improve our ability to do something well. This is not just about job performance, although that is an important area in which to build competence. But here I am discussing core competencies as a human, the core skills that make it easier to face life with confidence even in the midst of stressful times. No one is perfect at these skills, but everyone can continue to get better at them. Let's explore some of these.

Self-Awareness

Confident people understand their own emotions and thoughts and how they influence our behaviors. They have an attitude of openness to examine what they are thinking and doing and why. The skills in self-awareness include being able to identify and name emotions, recognizing their own strengths, acknowledging their own limitations, and believing they can accomplish what they set out to do.

Self-Control

Confident people can regulate their own emotions and behaviors, no matter what is going on around them. They have patience and can wait. They can plan and prioritize what they need to do, set goals and work toward accomplishing those goals, and filter out distractions and control their own impulses.

Effective Communication

Confident people have learned to communicate well. They can put their thoughts and needs into words in ways that others are willing to listen. They listen to others' thoughts and needs. They embody an attitude of respect, attentiveness, and caring. The skills include active listening, reflection, seeking to truly understand, and the use of neutral language to express concerns.

Social Awareness

Confident people are aware of others; they recognize the needs others may have and can understand other perspectives. They are willing to listen to others' needs. They have an attitude of respect and appreciation that we are all different and are all valuable. The skills of social awareness include empathy, kindness, gentleness, and respect.

Connections

Confident people are connected to others, knowing that we all need others to support and encourage us and we need to support and encourage others. They recognize that others have perspectives and skills that will add richness to their lives. The attitudes are respect, friendliness, and humility. The skills include caring, listening, cooperation, commitment, working through conflicts, and being supportive.

Conflict Resolution

Confident people are good at conflict resolution. They can calmly listen to the other person's concerns, seeking to understand why this is an issue and how they are being affected by it. They respectfully ask questions to clarify the details so it can be fully understood. Then they ask the other party to listen to their side. At that point, both sides can work toward a mutually beneficial resolution—or at least agree to disagree. The attitudes are respect, humility, and concern. Skills of conflict resolution include patience, active listening, and calmness.

Making Wise Decisions

Confident people take the time to make wise decisions. They think about the possible positive or negative consequences of the choices before them and are aware of the long-term effects of their choices. They also take into consideration how their decisions affect others. They are willing to take responsibility for their decisions and their outcomes. The attitudes are consideration, attentiveness, and thoughtfulness. The skills include reflection; identifying problems, resources, and situations; and moving toward effective solutions.

Ever Learning and Growing

The first step to increasing your competence is to understand we always have room to grow and improve. When you recognize there are areas for improvement in your life, you will continue to grow more competent. Competency is not a destination we arrive at; it is a journey we are ever learning and growing toward. When we quit learning, in some ways, we start dying. No matter what we already know, a competent person finds ways to improve on a daily basis.

Here are a few easy ways to improve your competence.

- Consider every difficulty an opportunity; within it is a seed of growth. When you approach every circumstance with a positive attitude—your whole life becomes a learning opportunity.
- Find social connections who are seeking to grow and become more competent. When you are friends with people who are smarter and more competent than you, you will grow in your own competence.
- Be a mentor. As you help others to grow to become more competent, your own competency will increase.
- Use your time wisely. Take advantage of opportunities to learn new things. Explore. Be curious.
- Pay attention to what you love to do. Sometimes when you love doing something, you might overlook the fact that you have a confident talent and skill there.

Fear of Failure

Gaining skills leads toward confidence, but sometimes people are afraid to try something new. What keeps them from gaining new skills is the fear of failure. They are afraid they will make a mistake and not be able to do it right, and other people won't like it or them because of their failure. Let me tell you a secret. All of us fail. There is not one human being on the planet right now who has succeeded every time they started to do something new. The reason adults can risk failure is that they know that failure just means that this thing didn't work this time. Failure does not mean I'm a human being with no value. I have the right to make mistakes. You could say that the only people who rarely fail are those who never do anything. If you try anything new, you are less likely to fail. Except then you are failing at growing into mature competent life.

Fear of Not Being Good Enough

Sometimes it's a sense of inferiority that keeps people from trying to learn new skills. They might feel like they are not good enough or smart enough. Let me tell you a secret. You don't have to be the best at everything to bring value to the world. Just do what is in front of you to do. In the world's sports games, only one can win the gold medal. But the rest of life is different, you do not have to be the very best at everything to have significance. Even those gold medal-winning athletes are not the best at everything—only at that thing, and they may be good at many other things and maybe only tolerable at a few things. A lot of people can be really good at something, and that is wonderful. However, it's important to be realistic about goals. Not everyone can win a marathon, and that's fine! If you like to run and follow that goal it will develop in your characteristics and skills that will help in other parts of your life. You could be better today at sticking to things that are not easy, you can become better at caring about others than you were yesterday. You can build skills every day. If we don't do things just because we're not the best, the world is losing the value we could have been bringing to the world. We need what you bring to the world.

In Summary

It is easy to feel confident when we have skills and competence. We can learn new skills and develop competence as our talents and strengths are recognized and built up. Being good at trying is a helpful skill. We work through difficult problems and mistakes, expanding our knowledge and skill along the way; our accomplishments are the result of a combination of ability, effort, study, training, practice, and experience. Core competencies as a human make it easier to face life with confidence even in the midst of stressful times. No one is perfect, but everyone can continue to get better.

CHAPTER 5

Confident Decision-Making

The Right Decisions for the Right Reasons

Making confident decisions knowing you are doing the right things for the right reasons. This happens best when we understand the values that drive our decisions. A major part of building confidence is knowing what is essential to you. What are the values you hold dear?

We were handed our first values by our parents and the other important adults in our lives when we were children. As we matured, we studied the values of our parents, our people, our nation, and our world, we made decisions about what kind of person we wanted to be. Examining and choosing our own values is a part of the solid core that confident people have.

Aspirational Values vs Behavioral Values

You will hear people say, "Do as I say, not as I do." An appropriate response to that is, "What you do speaks so loud, I can't hear what you say." Aspirational values are the values we *say* we hold to. Behavioral values are the ones we *demonstrate* by the things we do and the choices we make. There are many values that drive our behaviors and our decision-making.

> For a FREE resource - Go to FaithfulHabits.com/ TraumaHealingSeries
>
> For a Values Guide, a list and description of more than 100 values

A major part of building confidence is knowing what values you hold dear. Values have a major influence on a person's behaviors and attitudes and serve as broad guidelines in choosing what actions are best to do or what way is best to live. Examining our own values and choosing our own values is a part of the solid core that confident people have. Next, we will explore how to make confident decisions using your values as a guide.

Let's take a look at the way our decisions are made when it comes to either working for a company or being self-employed. First, we need to look at our values in two important areas: our money and our time. What are your monetary values? To get rich? To be independently wealthy? To have enough money to get by? Do you want to live comfortably and take care of your family? Or have enough money to be generous to others?

*Those who work their land will have
abundant food, but those who chase
fantasies will have their fill of poverty.*
Proverbs 28:19

What about your values surrounding time? Is recreational time important to you? Being able to do what you want with your time is a facet of valuing freedom. Lots of people who are self-employed have a strong freedom value. But there is a tradeoff. I have been self-employed for a major part of my life. The way I describe it is, when you are self-employed, you get to work any 80 hours of the week you want. I always say that with a little chuckle, but I mean it. Being self-employed means you have the sole responsibility for whether your work will succeed or fail.

When you are self-employed, you are free to make your own decisions about what you're going to do, when you're going to do it, and how you're going to do it. But that is informed by what your customers want. Being self-employed means you're producing a product or service for a customer, and that customer gets to buy it or not buy it, so you have to meet the need of your customer in order to stay in business. Additionally, you have lots of things to do you may not enjoy doing. For example, not everyone enjoys marketing, but when you are self-employed, if you don't market, you may not have any customers to do work for.

However, part of that 80 hours of working happens while you are puttering around in the garden having fun out in your yard, while also thinking about how to market your work. So are you working or are you not when you're out in your garden? When I say any 80 hours of the week you want, I count the planning time.

There is such a pleasure in having the freedom of being your own boss. I've always considered that to be a desirable aspect. For me, the value of this freedom outweighs the value of a steady paycheck.

What about your values around money and work? Is having a constant, reliable income a high value for you? Then being self-employed may not be a good choice. Self-employment is, by its nature, a feast or famine job. Sometimes you have lots of income and sometimes you do not. In order to survive, you have to figure out how to live with regular bills and sporadic income. If that is too much of a stressor for you, then working for somebody else for a stable income is a better choice. What you give up for that stability is some of the freedom that you would have if you're self-employed.

To make a confident decision about employed versus self-employed, you examine whether your freedom value is stronger than your financial stability value. Knowing which you value most makes your decisions about work easier. When you make this decision intentionally, it may not be as stressful to do what your employer tells you to do, since it means getting a steady income and you decided that was your priority.

When you know what your basic values are, you can make confident decisions.

Doing the Right Thing

Mature, confident adults do what they know to be right whether or not they get the approval of the other people around them. When they have integrity, they have the approval inside of themselves that what they are doing is right. They have the evidence of why it is right and know it goes along with their values. Integrity means to be honest and upright, someone you can trust. When you have integrity, people can rely on you. You are consistently responsible and all of who you are is integrated in all your life. Who you are on Sunday morning at church is the same as who you are at a Friday night party. You have the confidence of being whole and fit for your purpose.

Priorities as a Guide to Decision-Making

When you sort out your values and what your priorities are, it gives you the confidence to be able to say no when you need to say no and yes where you need to say yes. Your confidence comes from spending time working out your decision-making matrix. When I make decisions in line with my values, I can have confidence that I've made the right decision, even if it is not a comfortable or easy decision.

My priorities tell me in what order I need to assign each task or decision. When my values are to care for my family, and that includes keeping stable housing for them, then my priorities in spending money reflect this. Paying the rent takes priority above buying a game to play, or new clothes, or a fancy dinner out.

Values and Your Loyalties

Your values also affect your loyalties. What's your highest priority for loyalties in your life? For instance, my highest priority is to be faithful to God. My priority to God is higher than my priority for family and friends, even though family and friends are a very high priority in my life. How does that play out?

I had a dear friend call me out of the blue in the middle of the week and ask what I was doing. Then she said, "Could you take me to the emergency room?" I responded, "Yes. I'll be right there," and I hung up the phone and drove right over to her house. She said later she was surprised I didn't even ask why she needed to go. I didn't need to know why my friend needed to go to the ER. I am loyal to my friend. If my friend needs to go to the emergency room, I'm going to drop everything and go. Tell me about it on the way there. I knew she wouldn't ask me frivolously.

But my loyalty has limits because of my priorities. If I have a friend who asks me to lie for them, or who asks me to do something wrong, I'm going to say no because my loyalty to my faith, to my God, and therefore to truth, has a higher priority than my loyalty to family or friends. My family and friends know this and therefore wouldn't ask me to do those things.

Lifestyle Decisions

How does your lifestyle reflect your values? Sometimes there are areas that we are trying to grow in. If generosity is one of your values, does the way you spend your time show generosity? Does the way you spend your money show generosity? Does the way you take out the garbage and pick up your own messes show generosity? These are behaviors we can grow into. If our aspirational value is to be someone who is generous, then we have to think about the behaviors that go with a generous heart. It is one thing to hand out money, but it is another to grow our heart to be generous in all of our life. If we have trained our heart, attitude, and thoughts to be generous, our behaviors will follow that.

In Summary

Making confident decisions is when you know you are doing the right things for the right reasons. Confident people make decisions to do what they know to be right whether or not they get the approval of the other people around them. Our values are our guide to making confident decisions.

CHAPTER 6

Confidently Evaluating My Decisions

One of the most significant ways to build your confidence is by understanding the "why" of your life and everything you do. When you take a new job, make a big decision, or start a new project, ask yourself why you are doing this. What is the bigger reason behind your actions? Knowing your "why" gives you the confidence that your judgment is solid.

A component of having confidence in knowing you are doing the right things for the right reasons. In the previous chapter, we explored how our values can give us a template for making good decisions. Here, we will learn how to evaluate the decisions we make. Sometimes information, understanding, or circumstances may change, and we need to look again at the decisions we made and why in order to sustain our confidence that we are doing the right thing.

When we don't have confidence anytime we are wrong can feel like a threat to our competence, or even to our very existence.

A Threat to Our Existence

Is being wrong a slight annoyance or a threat to existence? Some people respond to being told they are wrong as if it's a threat to their existence. If they feel that the only way they have value in the world is because they are right, and their beliefs are the only beliefs that are right. To be told they are wrong feels to them like a threat to their very existence or right to breathe air on the planet. Therefore, they will fight very strongly to prove they are right—perhaps even after they've been proven that they are wrong.

One of the things we know as confident adults is that being wrong is an annoyance or an inconvenience, but it is not a threat to our existence. Well, perhaps if your opinion is that we could jump out of an airplane at 30,000 feet without a parachute with no ill effect, then being wrong could be a threat to your existence. But most of the time, when we are wrong, it just means that something needs to change, and we change it. To make confident decisions we look at the available information and resources we have, evaluate our values and priorities, and decide. If something changes we can re-evaluate and make a new decision, or re-affirm the one we made with confidence.

How Do We Know Right from Wrong?

As we discussed elsewhere in this Trauma Healing Series, there are a number of standards by which we can evaluate right and wrong. When we say something is wrong, a question to ask ourselves is "Wrong according to what standard?"

- Is it wrong according to a legal standard?
- Is it wrong according to a moral standard?
- Is it wrong according to a biblical standard?
- Is it wrong according to an ethical standard? Which one?
- Is it wrong according to a standard of competency?
- Is it wrong according to a personal preference standard?

For example, if the window glass gets washed and it has streaks all over it we would say that the window was washed wrong. But it is not illegal to leave streaks on a window. It is not immoral to leave streaks on the glass. The Bible does not discuss the washing of window glass. It is not unethical way to wash a window. But according to the professional competency standards of window washing, leaving streaks is wrong. And perhaps it is also wrong according to personal preference.

So, when we say something is wrong it is good to stop and think, wrong according to what standard. Sometimes when we state something is wrong we are stating our own personal preference standard. If I say all walls should be off-white and you say some walls should have a vibrant color, neither of us is wrong, and neither of us is right.

It is a matter of personal choice, of personal preference. It is not illegal, it is not immoral, nothing is scripture to decide it and it is not even a competency issue. Where it can become wrong is if we try to force our own personal preference into areas that are not our responsibility. When we are trying to tell other people what to do with their own decisions.

Self-evaluation Process

When I evaluate my own choices, it is good to look deeply into not only what I did, but also what I wanted, and what led to this outcome. Then I can confidently look at the strength of my choices or the things I need to change.

Here is the evaluation process I use.

- What happened?
  - This is an objective description of the events. At this step, keep it to neutral description.
- What choices were before you?
  - What were the possible outcomes of each choice?
- What did you choose to do?
  - What were you thinking?
- What were the effects of your choice?
  - Internally, what was the effect inside of you?

> o Externally, how did the result of this choice affect you today and in the future?
> o Others, what effect did this choice have on other people?

- What did you want?
- If necessary, what is my plan to change?

Let's look at an example where I showed up late to attend a meeting. We will work through this evaluation step by step, paying attention to what decisions were made that affected the outcome, and when the decisions were made.

What happened?

I showed up late to a meeting.

Why was I late?

When was the choice to be late made?

- I chose to listen to a person in stress instead of leaving from home on time.
- But why didn't I have time earlier to listen? Because I chose to cut all the calm buffer time (30 minutes) out of my schedule that morning.
- What did I want in the moment: To rest longer. I chose to lay in bed an extra 30 minutes, I felt tired and wanted to rest.
- But why was I extra tired? I chose to go to bed two hours later than usual. I chose to be engaged in external entertainment media instead of going to bed on time.
- What core need was I trying to fulfill? Freedom.

- Why was I feeling a drive for freedom? Because I chose to overwork earlier that day. At home I wanted to have some down time!
- Why did I choose to overwork? Because I wanted to be diligent, dependable, to control the daily workload situation.

The choice to be late to that meeting was actually made the day before, when I let my work/life balance become over work loaded.

What were the results of my choice?

Being late to the meeting.

I violated my own values of being diligent, kind, compassionate, and dependable.

What effect did my choice have on the environment?

Internally, I felt disappointed with myself for violating my own values.

Externally, I interrupted the focus and attention of the room and the meeting facilitator when I entered late. I unkindly broke their train of thought, therefore inconveniencing everyone in the room.

When you take the time to evaluate your own choices and the results of your choices, you are giving yourself the opportunity to make wiser, more confident choices in the future. Many of the smartest people in history failed many times before they succeeded. If you beat yourself up every time you make a mistake, you will feel too bruised and weary to try again.

An important skill of a confident person is to try new things, examine and evaluate how things are working, then modify and go again. If it did not turn out the way you hoped, it doesn't mean you don't have value. It just means you were wrong. It is important not to beat yourself up about past choices. Just look, examine, learn from them, and go on.

Have realistic expectations of yourself. If something goes wrong, use it as a lesson. Treat yourself the way you'd treat a friend who experienced a setback—with love and kindness. When you dwell on your mistakes, you remain stuck in your limiting thoughts. Keep moving forward one small step at a time and choose to steer clear of negative thoughts.

When you keep things in perspective, you let the small things roll off your back. You have the ability to find humor in situations that might cause others to get angry or defensive. Look for the light at the end of the tunnel and don't focus on one bad situation. Even small steps will boost your confidence. Don't take it personally when someone is rude or behaves badly. That is under their control, not yours; it is a reflection of their character, not yours.

In Summary

Build your confidence is by understanding the "why" of your life and everything you do. What is the bigger reason behind your actions? Knowing your "why" gives you the confidence that your judgment is solid and you are doing the right things for the right reasons. Understand which standard measures what is right or wrong. Evaluate your decisions, learn from them, and move on.

PART TWO

Having Contentment

When you have contentment, you are at ease with yourself and your life. You know how to ask for what you want, and you know how to make decisions that respect your values and the values of others. You are aware of your influence in the world. There is a deep freedom in contentment, a sense of knowing your place in the world. Contentment is an attitude of heart that you can develop. Contentment is not the fulfillment of what you want but rather the realization of what you already have.

CHAPTER 7

Asking for What I Want

Contentment is realizing how much I already have. Many times when I feel a need for something if I look around first at what I already have I may find that I need fewer things than I thought. But there are times when I need something and I need to ask some else for what I need.

Ask and It Will Be Given You

What do you really want? How will you get what you want unless you ask for it?

Ask and it will be given to you;
seek and you will find;
knock and the door will be opened to you.
For everyone who asks receives;
the one who seeks finds;
and to the one who knocks, the door will be opened.
Matthew 7:7, 8

You could read this passage to say that anything I ask for I'm going to get, but that's not been my experience. It's been my experience that when I ask in accordance with God's will, I might get what I asked for. However, other times, I don't know what I really want or need, and he gives me what I need instead.

> *Trust in the Lord and do good;*
> *dwell in the land and enjoy safe pasture.*
> *Take delight in the Lord,*
> *and he will give you the desires of your heart.*
> Psalm 37:3, 4

> *This is the confidence we have in approaching God:*
> *that if we ask anything according to his will,*
> *he hears us. And if we know that he*
> *hears us—whatever we ask— we know*
> *that we have what we asked of him.*
> 1 John 5:14, 15

These passages don't mean God is a vending machine, where I can ask for anything that I want and it's going to show up on my doorstep. When we ask things that are according to his will, he will answer us, but if we're asking for stuff just to waste it on our wants, he may not send us what we're asking for. However, I'd rather he didn't send me anything that's going to lead me away from him. I trust his will and trust that anything I should have will be given to me.

Asking the Right Person

When you want something, do you know who is the right person to ask? Who has the authority to give you an answer? Do you know why it is in the best interest of the other person to say yes? When you are looking to get a positive answer to a request, think about why it is in the best interest of the other person to give you a positive answer. What is the effect going to be for them if they say yes or if they say no? How is it going to affect their ability to do their jobs or meet their needs? Is there a way they can say yes to what you want, and it will be beneficial to their goals and their needs? If you think through what you want from someone else's perspective, sometimes all it takes to get the yes you want is reframing your need to prove it's beneficial for everybody involved.

Think of possible objections to what you want and the answer to those objections. If you think through these objections ahead of time, you can have the answers ready, making it harder for the person you're asking to say no.

How to Ask Clearly and Politely

When you're asking somebody for something, it's good to ask at the right time. When somebody is stressed and in the middle of something might not be the best time to make your request. Part of thinking about what the other person needs is thinking about whether they need time to consider your request. If so, maybe it will be good to put your request in writing and give it to them, so they have time to think about it. Often when people have to give an instant answer, their easy answer is to say no. When you give them time and write down the benefits they would experience if they said yes to you, it helps them to be able to give you the answer you want.

What Is Your Underlying Need?

Sometimes we have thought about why it would be good for the person we asked, we asked at the right time, we were asking the right person, and the answer is still no. At this point, we need to think about how to accept a no or not now gracefully. It's likely this is not the only time you're going to be asking someone for something, and if you accept no gracefully—you don't make a big deal out of it and you show that you understand that they have reasons they can't meet your request right now—they're going to have a lot nicer feeling toward you than if you try to guilt, pressure, or nag them to give you an answer. That gives them a bad feeling about you, and then the next time you ask for something you're more likely to hear no just because they're not fond of you because of how badly you treated them.

Asking for the Reason for No and Addressing the Concerns

When you get no for an answer ask why. Who will be negatively affected if you get what you want? If you understand the reason you can reassess your need and think about is there a different amount, a different way, at a different time rework your request trying to be focused more on what would be beneficial for them to say yes to you and maybe rework your request and then wait an appropriate length of time waiting for another opportunity to ask again.

Asking for what I want means I need to be aware of how what I'm asking for is going to affect my life and the lives of others around me. I need to remember I'm making a request for something I would like to have, not demanding something. I'm open to whatever the answer is going to be. For example, if you want to sleep in an extra hour one day a week, and you live in a house with other people, you can ask them to let you sleep in. If the garbage truck comes early on that day and you are usually up and take the waste bins out for collection, are you expecting someone else to do that? Maybe their answer is no, they don't want to do that. So keep your calm and contentment you look at your options: maybe pick another day to sleep in? Or are you putting the garbage out the night before?

Having contentment is learning to be able to be content whether you have much or little, whether you get what you ask for or whether you don't. Contentment is an attitude of heart, as is discontentment. Contentment is deciding that even though I may not be able to get what I want or need, I can still choose to be kind, thoughtful. and grateful for all the abundance I do have.

In Summary

How will you get what you want unless you ask for it? When you ask, are you aware of how your request will affect yourself and others, now and in the future? When we ask for what we want it is good to be clear and direct. Also to learn to want what is good and beneficial for yourself and others. Asking in line with God's will and the needs of others also considered will give you the best chance of getting what you want. And if the final answer is no, contentment is about giving up on wanting that.

CHAPTER 8

Contentment with Resources

Each of us has a lot of resources. Your resources are any assets you can draw on in order to fulfill a purpose or need or to function effectively, something from which a benefit is produced, and that enhances the quality of your life. Resources are a means of accomplishing something, including a source of strength or ability within yourself. We can be content with our resources, or we can be dissatisfied and always striving for what we don't yet have. Think about these words from the Apostle Paul to Timothy.

But godliness with contentment is great gain. For we brought nothing into the world, and we can take nothing out of it. But if we have food and clothing, we will be content with that. Those who want to get rich fall into temptation and a trap and into many foolish and harmful desires that plunge people into ruin and destruction. For the love of money is the root of all kinds of evil. Some people, eager for money, have wandered from the faith and pierced themselves with many griefs.

1 Timothy 6:6-10

To be content with resources is about learning to recognize the resources you already have, valuing them for the benefit they can bring to your life and the lives of others. Remember, all material resources are temporary. When people focus on money as the most valuable resource, it plunges them into a discontented life that does not end well. In their drive to get rich, they can lose sight of more important resources like integrity, family, health, and time.

Common Resources:

- **Money** is one of our resources. It has no value of its own. It is only paper or metal, or numbers in a ledger. Its value is in how it lets us have access to other resources. The value of money is not about how much we have; it's about how we manage what we have to bring benefit to ourselves and others. We can save money for present and future needs.

- **Time** is a resource more precious than money. Each day you have exactly as much time as the day before. You have exactly as much time as every other person on the planet. You can't save up time, but you can learn to work and live more efficiently so you have more time to do the important things you want to do.

* **Energy** and our physical strength is a resource that can grow if we're in good physical condition. We can increase or decrease our energy resources by our daily habits. Every day, we make choices about sleep, food, how we move, and how we handle the stress that increases this resource or lowers it.

* **Integrity** and your reputation are valuable resources. These guide your behavior and your choices. They help your life have strength and direction. They allow relationships and trust to grow with other people. And, perhaps most importantly, they give you a sense of peace within yourself.

* **Knowledge** is a resource. This is a resource we can increase daily. Have you learned something new today? Having the habits of a lifelong learner makes your mind more active. You see how things are connected and can make wiser decisions. Knowledge is a resource we benefit from ourselves, and we can share with others.

* **Skills** are a valuable resource. You have many skills and can constantly learn more. What do you know how to do well? Are you a good friend? A good parent? Do you know how to clean a house, drive a vehicle, shop for groceries? What job skills do you have? Can

you show up on time, do what your boss wants to be done, get along with co-workers?

- **Social Network.** The ability to make and keep friends is a skill. Family and friends enrich our lives. We bring value to their lives, and they bring value to our lives. When I need to know something, I may have a friend who has skills in that area. They can help me, and I have skills that can help them.

- **Material things** are helpful when we have enough for our needs. They can enhance the quality of our life. But how much stuff do you need? When we gather stuff for stuff's sake it begins to clutter our lives and hinder us from being able to do what is beneficial. The irony of stuff is enough enhances our lives, too much hinders our lives.

Your Resources, Your Responsibility

We all have many more resources than I have listed here. What all our resources have in common is it is our responsibility to manage and use them. When we focus on a resource as an end goal, it takes us out of balance. Like loving money for money's sake, rather than using money as a tool to bring value to your own life and the lives of others. Having material things is useful—until you have so many they have drained all your money and they steal your time and energy to care for them. You are responsible for the choices you make.

Contentment is about the wise use of what you have and being able to enjoy the benefits these resources bring without getting caught up in the dissatisfaction of always grasping for more. How we manage our resources says a lot about what we deem as important in our lives. Being responsible with resources and planning ahead gives you a calmer, more content life. Living within, or even a little below, your income brings freedom from want. Having a priority template in line with your values makes decisions about resource use easy.

I am not saying this because I am in need, for I have learned to be content whatever the circumstances. I know what it is to be in need, and I know what it is to have plenty. I have learned the secret of being content in any and every situation, whether well fed or hungry, whether living in plenty or in want. I can do all this through him who gives me strength.

Philippians 4:11-13

In Summary

Each of us has access to many resources. We can be content with what we have, or we can be dissatisfied and always wanting more. Contentment with resources is about the wise use of what you have, as well as learning to recognize the resources that you have, valuing them for the benefit they can bring to your life and the lives of others. Remember that all material resources are temporary. Abundance is about a mental attitude of recognizing that you do have more than you need.

CHAPTER 9

Contentment in Social Relationships

What does it mean to be content in relationships with family, friends, co-workers, bosses, and casual acquaintances? To start with, there is an absence of a lot of common conflicts. When you have contentment, you are at ease with yourself and your life and at ease with those around you. When we feel contentment, we accept people for who they are and don't spend our time trying to get them to change to how we want them to be. Therefore, a lot of conflict goes away. People are different than you. They have different ways of seeing the world and different opinions about what is important. In those very differences is a wider and richer view of the world. Contentment in social relationships means we respect their right to be different, and we treat them with respect.

Contentment in Social Relationships

We all gain from being socially connected. In healthy, contented connections, we grow closer to others and the natural side effect of that closeness is that we gain access to the knowledge, skills, information, and connections that other people have. It is part of the richness of connections. We may have common interests and there is a mutual back-and-forth sharing and benefit. Also, it is good to connect with others that have different interests. Contentment brings us into the joy of learning new things, being exposed to new places, meeting new people, and finding delight in this broadening of our world. In these relationships, the differences may make us the person who is learning and gaining more by the volunteered times, skills, and resources of the ones who know more and do more than we can. And we are the more knowledgeable one in some of these connections, gladly sharing resources, skills, and knowledge. That is the normal give-and-take of contented connections.

Healthy connections and friendships are motivated by enjoying each other's company, not just one person using the friendship to gain resources, status, or connections from another, then cutting off the connection when there is no more benefit. That was not a friendship; it was a using buddy. They were only connected as long as they could use the other for their own benefit.

Respecting

Contentment is a way of respecting yourself and others. Respect is polite behavior, treating people in a positive manner that acknowledges them for who they are, and giving due regard for their feelings, wishes, rights, or traditions. When we are content with ourselves and others, we are free to learn more about what makes each individual unique and seek to understand more about how they see the world. When we give up our need to change someone else, there is a peace in the relationship. They do not have to defend themselves against you and therefore they may seek to understand you more.

Contentment with others is a learned skill. As I get to know a person better, my level of respect for them may raise or lower depending upon how they behave and how they treat me, and what I learn about them. But my level of contentment with who they are is about how I have trained myself to see them as unique and valuable individuals, as they are. I can be curious about their motivations, their values, and their worldview. Contentment does not mean I have to agree with them. Also, I may set up protective boundaries with those who are not safe, and I may choose not to be in their company any more than necessary.

Contentment with People and Their Things

Contentment is about realizing how blessed we are to have these resources available to us. We enjoy the benefits of these resources while treating them with care to keep them in good shape for others to be able to use as well. Our true enjoyment and pleasure in using these resources is evident to the people around us and can also add to their enjoyment. We share a pleasure generously together and not just for our own use.

Contentment is a choice you make about how you treat other people when things are not going to your liking. When you are tired, frustrated, and feeling upset. When the other person is not helping you resolve your problem. That is a time to be extra careful to treat people with respect. It can be tempting to lose your contentment and take your frustration out on the person with unkind words and an aggressive attitude. But that will not help you get your needs met and you will let the situation erode your contentment and happiness. Handling the situation with grace, in a civil and polite way, will make everyone's day a little easier. You can keep an attitude of gratefulness for what you do have that is to your liking while you pursue what you need.

How we treat the people who disagree with us shows a great deal about our character and the level of respect we have for people in the world. If we only treat those who agree with us well, how are we different than the people that we don't respect? Even they do that.

Differing Opinions

Part of maturity is being able to respect where someone is and the opinions they have. We do not have to agree in order to respect. When we are content in ourselves, we are free to be content with where someone else is as well. We are free to listen to and share differing opinions politely.

Sometimes there are issues we need to address with people. It is possible to have awkward conversations politely and civilly. Yes, it will feel uncomfortable to have awkward conversations. But to avoid that awkward conversation may also leave you in an uncomfortable place, whereas if you have the conversation, you may have the possibility that things will get better. They may make it worse, true. Or they may change and become tremendously better. Taking the time to work through an awkward spot may mean that you will get the issue resolved and get back to your feeling of contentment sooner.

It is possible to disagree with someone's opinion firmly and assertively without disrespecting the person. The powerful way to disagree is to keep the disagreement to the points in the opinion and not to let it descend into judging and condemning somebody's character. We can seek to have unity without having uniformity. Unity is where we're all going in the same direction. Uniformity is where everybody looks alike, thinks like, believes alike, and has the same opinions. When we have unity and we're all going in the same direction and yet we have different opinions and beliefs, and we look different from one another, it brings a richness to life. There's a depth that is lacking when everything is the same.

Accepting that all people are different and that all people have value is an important part of having contentment in social relationships. Accepting that things will not be done just exactly like you want them done, and yet it is still okay, adds greatly to your contentment.

In Summary

To be content in relationships with family, friends, co-workers, bosses, and casual acquaintances is to accept people for who they are and not spend our time trying to change them. Accepting that all people are different and that all people have value is an important part of having contentment in social relationships. When we are appreciative of the differences we see in others, our contentment grows.

CHAPTER 10

Contentment in Parenting

As a parent, I have pondered the difference between vision and fantasy. It is a good thing to have a vision of what life could be like for your children, but we lose our contentment as parents when we have expectations of what our children must be like. As a young mother, I wanted to challenge and encourage my child. I tried to remember to be grateful to God for who my son is and not chase some silly fantasy of who I wanted him to be.

It is important not to get vision and fantasy mixed.

I have learned how to give up what I can't keep, or never really had, so I can enjoy what I have been given. An ideal fantasy and vision often look and feel the same on the surface. Both consist of mental pictures or images of good ideals—except one is a projection of my own ego, and the other is the product of humble pondering. How can we tell the difference? There is no sure way. We all stumble through, making mistakes along the way.

When I thought about what I wanted my son to grow into I saw the image of a mature Christian man: dedicated to God, with a heart for ministry, intelligent with a love of learning, sensitive to the needs of others, a healthy sense of self-worth. A man who is comfortable with himself: whether the work is laboring in the fields or leading some huge organization. What part of this is a vision of the character traits I could encourage and help develop in my son and what part of the image was envy or a fantasy of my ego? Envy is when I see traits in someone else's child and wish my child were like that. Envy is common among parents.

I had to remember that this child was entrusted to my care for a short period of time; ultimately God decides what happens to him. When my fantasy image did not work, I began to doubt my ability to parent at all, as if I got myself into this and God is not around. When I realize that God is my source, I could relax, feel content in the simple principles of parenting: love him, communicate with him, have fun with him, teach him the Word of God, and pray for him. Whenever I find myself disappointed, when something does not meet my expectations, I stop and look; was my expectation a part of the vision or a fantasy?

Vision vs. Fantasy

An ideal fantasy image works only in a perfect fantasy world; a vision works in an ordinary, unpredictable world. A fantasy image can fit perfectly into my well-constructed daydreams. Vision never comes with all the answers. Vision is, by definition, seeing something beyond the present possibilities, so it never seems as if it's going to work, but vision works even in my fractured life and that of my son. An ideal fantasy emerges from an egocentric, self-established image of parenting; a vision emerges from thoughtful, loving prayer. The ideal image of the fantasy child can become a standard to fail against; a vision for my child can become a positive goal to aim for. If I become lost in the fantasy of the child of my dreams, I can miss the blessing of the child I have.

When I grasp to control everything, not only do I lose my contentment, I also do not have control! Having control, especially total control, is a fantasy. A lot of things we only have influence over, not control of.

We can effect change in others through the ways we affect others—influence, modeling, parenting, authority, etc. How are you influencing, for good or ill? All of us influence other people not just with our words but with our behavior and what we choose to do. People around us notice what we're doing, and it can affect them for good or for ill. When we raise our children, they are greatly affected by what they see in us. Some people say, "You do what I say, not what

I do." To which I answer, "What you do speaks so loud I can't hear what you said."

So much of a parent's power is the power of influence—what you do speaks loudly. You were greatly influenced by your parents, by the major caretakers in your life when you were growing up. You were around the people your parents allowed you to be around. You were influenced by the parents of the friends you had when you were growing up. In all of these adults, you saw a model of how to behave, how to handle stress, and how to handle conflict, and you internalized that.

Now, as an adult, you get to choose how content you will be, how you decide to handle conflict, how you decide to treat other people, how you decide to have respect and regard for other people around you, and how you decide to handle stress. If you don't take the time to look at what you're doing and why, you'll just repeat what was modeled for you. Now, if they were good influences, maybe it's not a problem to just embrace that and go on. But not all of us had the luxury of having good influences, or maybe we had good influences 80% of the time, but the other 20% is something we don't want to repeat in our lives. If you don't want to be that kind of person, you can make the choice to learn how to change.

The Consultant Role of Parents with Adult Children

From adult to adult, we can be available to offer consultation when asked, but otherwise, we should let people make their own mistakes and find their own successes. A consultant is someone who answers the questions, who provides input when asked for input. They don't try to control what someone else is doing. We can offer to help them problem solve, humbly helping them explore what went wrong and what resources they have to move forward. We can rejoice with them in their successes.

It is important as parents to equip our children and then step back and let them succeed on their own. This is not something that happens all at once. It starts when they are little and at each stage of their development we encourage, teach, train, equip, and step back a little to let them succeed. The shift to consultant comes a little at a time. When we train young children we give a lot of direction, and also few choices. The purpose is to help them learn how to make good decisions. By the teen years, they have a lot more choices to make and we are in that transition to a consultant role.

When adults try to control their adult children, the children have to learn to set boundaries. Sometimes they set physical boundaries by moving thousands of miles away because they couldn't get the space they needed when they lived close by. If they have the social contentment they need in the relationship, the respect they need, and the autonomy they need several generations can live together in harmony, even in the same home. However, it requires that each one is respectful of the other's role and purpose.

In Summary

We can effect change in the world around us through the ways we affect others. This is seen most profoundly in the role of a parent with their children. We get to choose whether we affect others for good or ill. When we have an image of how we want our child to be that ideal image of the fantasy child can become a standard to fail against, but a vision for my child can become a positive goal to aim for. If I become lost in the fantasy of the child of my dreams, I can miss the blessing of the child I have. As parents, we equip our children and then step back into the contentment of watching them succeed in their own way.

CHAPTER 11

Freedom and Responsibility

What do freedom and responsibility have to do with contentment? If I have freedom, I would be content, right? When you have contentment, you are at ease with yourself and your life. There is a deep freedom in contentment. But freedom without responsibility can become just an excuse for selfish distain for other people's freedom. Those who have an abundance of money have a great many freedoms, and yet if they don't have contentment, their life is constrained and has limits that hinder their happiness due to valuing things or money too much. Contentment is freedom in itself. It allows us to do what we want when we want.

There are limits to our freedom. "The right to swing my fist ends where the other man's nose begins." The quote is from Supreme Court Justice Oliver Wendell

Holmes, Jr. As others have said, your rights are protected up to the point where you infringe on someone else's rights. Our freedom ends where another person's freedom begins. Being responsible puts a helpful framework around our freedoms so that they may be more fully enjoyed.

Being responsible means that people can count on you to do the next right thing. They can count on you being where you said you would be when you said you would be there. Other people never have to wonder or worry about where you are and what you are doing. Responsible people choose to be accountable for their own actions. Responsible people are content to take care of their own tasks and help out other people.

Contentment in Finances

Responsible money handling skills are important to contentment. The basic money skills of earning your own living, caring for your responsibilities, caring for those who depend on you, and having enough for your needs give you confidence. Once you get the most basic of needs met, contentment is not as much about how much money is brought into the family as it is about not spending more than what comes in. Confidence and contentment in money handling are about making choices to care for needs, having some for generosity and some for savings, then looking at what might be available for discretionary spending on things that are wanted.

Responsible money handling is about knowing where the resources are coming from and where they are going. Keep records so you know that information. Responsible people pay their bills on time. Responsible money handling includes setting aside a small amount each payday to build up an emergency fund.

Responsible Family Income Handling

Contentment in income handling begins with an attitude of valuing each member of the family. The adults provide for the needs of the family. Income and resources are spent in a way that benefits the needs of the family, not just one person. Take the example of a husband and wife with three very young children. One adult may work outside the home while the other one stays at home and cares for their children. The one income is spent on the needs of the family. It is not thought of as "my income" or "your income." It is thought of as "our income." They look at the family's expenses together. Resources are sorted out by needs as determined by both adults.

The adult who stays home is valued as equal to the one who brings in the cash. They know that if the family had to pay out money for child care, it would take most of the wages the second adult would bring in. But the main value is that the children are being nurtured by a loving parent, not by a paid worker. The quality of the children's lives is greatly benefited by the effort *both* parents are putting into the family. The needs of all the family members are considered as choices are made of how to spend the family income.

Choices

Whenever we have options, we get to choose if we do what is easy or what is right. They are not always the same thing. If we struggle to decide whether to choose A or B, it can help to use your values as a guide. Which choice is in line with your values, and which one drifts away from your values? Which choice is clearly right? Or, put another way, imagine yourself in a courtroom. You are in the witness chair. The prosecuting attorney is glaring at you and says sternly, "Why did you make that choice?" Which choice would you rather defend?

Sometimes both choices seem okay or at least almost okay. But Choice A I would have to explain in detail why that was the right choice, and Choice B I would not have to explain because it is just obviously the right choice. The reason I want to make choice A is because it is easier for me. But when I think of the courtroom scene, I would only want to defend choice B because it is obviously right. Therefore it is worth the little bit of extra effort it will take.

How Lack of Responsibility Affects Contentment

A lack of responsibility affects our contentment because it is a breaking of trust. Other people can feel like they need to be on their guard around you because you are not trustworthy. They cannot rely on the things you say and therefore do not pay much attention to you when you talk. The relationship is shallow and fragile. A lack of responsibility affects the contentment in our relationships in many ways. We can be content to accept people as they are, but the relationships tend to stay shallow and are easily broken. We do not invite untrustworthy people very deeply into our lives. Being responsible strengthens relationships because trust lets us risk getting close to people. They can rely on us, and we can rely on them.

Contentment is gratitude, appreciation, and acceptance of the way things are right now. It means to be happy with who you are, what you have, and where you are in life at this moment. It doesn't mean you are not seeking to make life better for yourself and others, it simply means you are aware of and enjoying the now as you work toward the future.

In Summary

There is a deep freedom in contentment. When you have contentment, you are at ease with yourself and your life. Being responsible puts a helpful framework around our freedoms so that they may be more fully enjoyed. Responsible people are content to take care of their own tasks and help out other people.

CHAPTER 12

Acceptance

Basic acceptance is when you understand that life will not always be to your liking. There is pain, discomfort, inconvenience, unfairness, and problems. Life has pain. That is just the reality of life. When you have solved what can be solved and checked your understanding of what remains, there are two choices left: suffer and be miserable, or accept that pain happens and figure out how to move forward anyway.

Acceptance is keeping our attitude of contentment even when life is not going our way. Acceptance is a learned skill that helps you to better be able to tolerate disappointment, pain, and discouragement without adding the suffering of bitterness, resentment, and destructive behaviors to it.

A lot of life is out of our control. Maybe most of it. Acceptance means we understand this truth. We are affected by circumstances we did not create; we have to go through pain and discomfort we cannot change. But we do not have to be trapped in misery. We suffer in misery when we fight against facts we cannot change. Acceptance of those facts does not mean that we agree with them, nor does it mean that we are helpless victims of them. We simply accept this is what is and actively decide what our response is going to be. Pain is inevitable; misery is optional.

Sadness, disappointment, pain, unfairness, and loss are a part of the reality of the human experience. No one wants to experience that pain; it is difficult to accept those hard realities. But fighting against reality will not keep it from being true. As difficult as it is to accept the reality of pain, when you attempt to avoid or resist uncomfortable emotions, you actually add suffering to your pain. You can stop the additional suffering by practicing acceptance. There are many life situations not in our control and where we will experience pain. We can't avoid that pain, but we can control how much we suffer through the experience. Suffering is the part we can control.

Observe vs Judge

Here is a two-part exercise that will just take a few minutes. First, take a couple of moments, look around you right now and write down a quick description of what you see, noticing the condition of the things.

For the second part, take just a moment, look at the description you wrote, underlining all the neutral describing words and circling all the negative judging, condemning words. What did you notice about how you talk to yourself about things?

Do you have that same pattern in thinking and talking about yourself and other people? When you allow yourself to be content with yourself and accept yourself as you are, you also learn to accept others as they are, flaws and all.

Too often, we look around at people and things and judge instead of observing. We look at all the ways that are short of perfection, or at least short of what we want. Then we slide right into judging worth and condemning the shortcomings. The effect of this on your own life is that you may find yourself living in misery in a world that constantly disappoints you. But the bulk of this misery is of your own making.

Acceptance is being able to observe how things are in neutral ways, not judging, not condemning. By noticing without judging, we become more aware of what is available to us. Acceptance is not a passive or apathetic view of the world. It is an intentional way of looking at the world and your place in it. Acceptance lets you enjoy the richness of the beauty around you every day. Your days are calmer and have less stress. From this peaceful, grateful place, you can look around at how you can make life better for yourself and others.

What it means to have contentment

Contentment is a state of happiness and satisfaction, being calm, and having peace of mind. It includes gratitude, appreciation, and acceptance of the way things are right now. It means to be happy with who you are, what you have, and where you are in life at this moment. Self-control is an attribute of contentment. A contented person is humble, respectful, and has self-discipline that restrains from doing wrong acts and does the next right thing. The abundance you see all around you is enough to lead a happy and healthy life. From the base of acceptance, you can choose to find fulfilling activities to bring value to the world. People experience good feelings when they achieve something they worked toward completing.

Circumstances Change

When my son was a little boy, I was the most important woman in the world to him. That was my place, my value in his world, as it should be. When he became an adult, he found a special young lady to love and commit his life to and they got married. She became the most important woman in the world to him. Now my place in his world is a little further back, as it should be.

As our children grow up, our role as parents shifts to helping them to make that transition to adulthood. As they grow into the responsibilities and freedoms of an adult our place in their lives diminishes, as it should. It is no longer about me and my choices. Now it is about their choices.

Acceptance of these changed circumstances allows me to grow into contentment in my new role. I need to respect their autonomy—their freedom to make their own choices—even when I think those choices are making their lives harder or if I think there could be better choices to make. That is not my place. If I am asked, I can consult on it and offer an opinion. But if I'm not asked, I need to stay out of it and let them live their own life.

In Summary

A lot of life is not under our control. Acceptance means we understand that we are affected by circumstances and discomfort we cannot change. We suffer in misery when we fight against facts we cannot change. When you attempt to avoid or resist things you cannot change, you actually add suffering to your pain. Acceptance is an attitude that lets you enjoy the richness of the beauty around you. When things change, we can accept the change and look for the positive in the new circumstances. That allows us to grow into contentment.

PART THREE

Abundance - Components of a Happy Life

In part two we discussed in depth what it means to have contentment in many different parts of life. When you allow yourself to be content with yourself and accept yourself as you are, you also learn to accept others as they are, flaws and all. When we understand our place in the world, accepting what cannot be changed, contentment is a natural consequence. From this foundation, we can then seek to change the things that can be changed to make the world better for ourselves and others. Here in part three, we will discuss the components of a happy life; we will look at how to bring more happiness into life.

An attitude of abundance does not rely on how much you have. It is a state of mind, as is happiness. Happiness is an enjoyable or satisfying feeling when life is pleasurable. It ranges from mild enjoyment to intense delight. Components of happiness include caring for your own physical, emotional, and mental needs; generosity, connections to family and a social community; bringing value to the world; having well-thought-out priorities; and cultivating a spiritual life, including connecting in a faith-based community. You can create a richness of life that goes far beyond the temporary rewards of success and create lasting happiness for yourself in any situation. Happiness is a step beyond contentment and is more long-term.

CHAPTER 13

Caring for Your Own Needs

A fundamental component of happiness is caring for your own basic needs. Our most basic needs are water, food, shelter, rest, and safety. If we don't have these needs met as a foundation, it is hard to even think about other needs. After the bare minimum in quality and quantity of these items, the question becomes, how much of each of these do we need to be happy?

Vital Components of a Happy Life

Before you will have resources to care for others—another vital component of happiness—you need to function well in the basic self-care skills of adulthood. You need to know how to care for your own needs. The following is not a list of all those basic skills, but it is a good start. These are not innate, but skills you learn by practice.

Physical Movement

What type of movement brings you joy? We are designed to move around physically. Those who have ever felt pain in movement, sprained a joint, or wrenched or twisted their ligaments, causing pain and swelling, know the happiness of when it heals, and they can again move without pain.

How do you move when you are happy? Do you dance, or run? Happiness in physical movement is about being aware of the wonder of how we walk and dance and move and then enjoying it. Part of caring for our own needs is treating our body with care and respect in the way that it needs so that pain and discomfort don't hinder our happiness.

Managing Your Money

Love of money is the root of all evil, but not handling money well is a cause of much unhappiness and stress. Knowing how to manage money well and handle a budget can keep money in its rightful place as a helpful resource rather than letting it get out of balance to create stress. This starts with the simple act of knowing how much is coming in and how much is going out. Most people find they feel happier knowing they have more coming in than going out. There is a calm pleasure in knowing you have some finances set aside for major costs that may come up. Saving money little by little is a very useful skill.

If we don't pay attention to how we handle it, money can just be frittered away, and then it is all gone, and we don't know where it went. The difference between an abundance mentality and a scarcity mentality is the choices we make on how we care for ourselves and others and how we handle our resources. If we have $100 coming in this week and we spend $120, we can feel like there is not enough. On the other hand, if we have $100 coming in and we spend only $80, we have $20 leftover and it can feel like we have an abundance.

Managing Your Time Wisely

Time is similar. If I fritter away time on social media or entertainment, then it can feel like I don't have enough time to do things. I can feel overwhelmed with all I am supposed to get done. Like with money, it leads to a scarcity mentality. But if I schedule out the things I have to do and get those done first, then I have relaxing time I can spend on self-care or entertainment or social media for fun, with no guilt. This margin provides a sense of abundance, even within the same amount of time.

Time-management skills are vital to caring for yourself and others. Being able to be where you need to be when you need to be there, and getting things done on time are all part of the structure that will put more peace in your life.

Getting Enough Sleep

In the world of confident, content, and happy adults, getting enough sleep is a strong component of caring for your own needs. Some people wish they could just sleep longer, if only they could sleep in. Actually, most people can—go to bed a little bit earlier at night.

Let go of this day's activities sooner. Set up a restful, calming nighttime routine an hour or so before you want to be asleep. Different people have different rhythms of wake-sleep, taking the effort to figure out what works best for you can be a helpful exercise.

Saying 'No' Respectfully

Saying NO when needed can save you a lot of time, confusion, guilt, commitments, and stress. There are important things in our lives that it may be difficult to get back—your time, your health, your virtue, your life. Don't treat those lightly. It's fine for people to ask. And it's just as fine for you to say "no." When we have good boundaries and feel confident to say no when we need to it adds to our happiness that we are able to have the freedom of yes and no in how we live our lives. We are free to do what is in line with our values.

Spending Time Alone

The skill to spend time alone and be good company for yourself is helpful to happiness. Yes, we need others, as I will discuss in the chapter on family and social connections, but we also need time alone with our own thoughts. We need the skill of entertaining ourselves without toys, electronics, or other people. Learning how to be good company for yourself gives you a strong and ever-present resource, adding to your ability to find pleasure and happiness.

Practicing Self-compassion

Be good to yourself. Especially when things don't go well, or you mess up or fail. Beating yourself up over your failures just makes you weary and is not productive. Think about the comforting things you would say to a friend in this kind of situation and say those things to yourself. By caring for yourself as you care for others you will have a better chance of a positive outcome, even through stressful situations.

Taking Basic Happiness for Granted

Think back to a time you felt really, really thirsty, and then you drank some water. Remember the feeling of refreshment? It was a pleasure to feel that relief. In my part of the world, we often take water for granted. We walk over to the nearby sink, turn on a faucet, and take as much clean, cool water as we want. To get clean, we step into a shower and turn on clean, warm water to wash our bodies. That is a basic level of a happy feeling that we take for granted. When we cease to be aware of the small pleasures around us each day, we let feelings of happiness slip away from us. To experience happiness in the water that we have is to be grateful for small but vital pleasures.

To find happiness in something as basic as water is to approach life like a little child. Take notice of the wonders around you and the delight they bring. Take a moment to think about food. Every day we eat food to survive. Pleasure in food is available to us every time we take a bite. Notice the colors, the aromas, the textures. Anticipation can enhance our pleasure. Or we can choose to find fault with the timing, the surroundings, or the quality. Whether we find happiness or unhappiness in food does not rely on the food in front of us, but on the attitude with we approach this food experience. Are we choosing to enhance our happiness or are we choose to throw away happiness with both hands?

Let us wrap this up segment about losing happiness by taking it for granted with a quick look at our place to live. If you have an attitude of gratefulness for having a roof over your head and protection from wind and rain, any place to live can add to your happiness. A lot of people are stuck in unhappiness about where they live because they don't like the neighborhood or the house or apartment they are living in. They don't like the little quirks in the house, the things that need to be repaired, or the things that are not working quite right. But if we take an inventory of how many things there are in our shelter that are good and be grateful for those, our happiness level raises. Do we have floors that keep us out of the dirt? Do we have windows that let light in? Thinking about those things that you are grateful for will have a major effect on your feelings of happiness or dissatisfaction.

In Summary

Caring for our needs is a vital component of a happy life. If we don't have these needs met as a foundation, it is hard to even think about other people or our other needs. Being aware of all the small pleasures around us enhances our feelings of happiness. We can let happiness drift away from us by an attitude of taking things for granted. Struggle and difficulty is a fact of life for everyone. Happiness is a choice; misery is optional.

CHAPTER 14

Family and Social Connections

Our family and social connections are vital components of our happiness. Who we consider our family is not solely blood relations, not just a social group made up of parents and their children or people descended from a common ancestor. Family can also consist of all the people who support and love us, the people we can confide in and trust. Our family can be large and growing.

Who Is My Family?

Family means having someone to love you unconditionally in spite of your shortcomings. Family is loving and supporting one another even when it's not easy to do so. Family is comfort; it is home. In the best case, we have our immediate family and our extended family. Family we grew up around and the family that we chose to put together ourselves.

People in a family have respect and appreciation for each other no matter how old, how young, where each one comes from, what they have experienced, where they are, how capable they are, how healthy they are, or who they love. Family is always there in good times and not so good times. Family includes all the people in our lives who commit to love and support us unconditionally. It is not a passive birthright but a choice we make of love, commitment, and kindness that helps us thrive both as individuals and as a family. Even when things go wrong, you can always depend on family. Family brings you back to your values and helps you make good decisions.

Disrupted Families

Not everyone has a loving family that they can be around. Some people have not had a nurturing biological family to grow up with. Family life for them was disrupted, and trauma, chaos, and trouble were their experience. That does not mean they have to be without family. They can build a new family of choice, people they choose to commit to and care for, people who care for them.

In my work with people who are healing from childhood trauma, I find that we all have a strong need to be connected to others, to feel a part of a family, a tribe, a people. I think it is part of how we are created. People seem drawn to love their parents—the people who raised them—no matter how those people treated them. When raised in a loving home, it's obvious that children would love their parents. But even with parents who were not easy to live with, where there was trauma in their relationship, there can still be a strong desire for family connection.

However, we can set boundaries with all the people in our lives. Boundaries define how much access to our lives each person has. With good people who bring positive things to our lives, the boundaries are fairly open, and they have a lot of access to our lives. That creates connection and happiness, that close bond we seek with other humans. When there are people it is not healthy for you to be around, even if they are blood family, you need to set safe boundaries, so contact and access to your life are more limited.

Social Connections

In addition to family, we have many other social connections. Friends are an important component of our happiness as well. There are different levels of relationships in our lives. Some people we connect with very closely and intimately, and some people we're more on a surface level with, but we are meant to be connected. As discussed in *Connections*, book three of the Trauma Healing Series, we need to be connected to people in all the different levels of friendship in our life. We especially need the close friends where we have deep connections, sharing our joys and our stresses, supporting and encouraging one another. We also need casual friends because they widen our perspective and enrich our life. It adds to our happiness as they bring other interesting things into our lives.

Diversity of Friendship

It enriches our happiness when we are connected with people who are different than ourselves. When you are with people who are just like you, you are losing out on a wider perspective of the world. Be careful to choose friends who share your core values because they encourage you to become better. They don't pull you away from your values. Outside of that, though, diverse friendships bring more interesting and happy things into your life.

So it is good to have

- Friends who are older than you
- Friends who are younger than you
- Friends who are that are in your same financial situation
- Friends who are in a different financial situation
- Friends who are the same ethnic background as you
- Friends who are a different ethnic background than you

When we are alone or when we are only with people who are just like us, we can grow lopsided. We need to be out and around the richness of the differences between people so our lopsidedness will get bumped off and we become more balanced and happier.

The Ebb and Flow of Happy Families

Another part of having close relationships with family and friends is knowing how to handle the struggles that come up. There will always be times when we hurt each other, intentionally or unintentionally. Happy families work through disagreements and do not let resentment fester, but resolve them and put them to rest. It adds to our happiness when we don't have unfinished business with family and friends. As much as it relies on you, be at peace with everybody. Ask for forgiveness and be willing to give forgiveness. Love overlooks a multitude of wrongs. Take the time and have the courage to work through things and put offenses to rest, whatever it takes, including seeing a counselor if necessary.

Accepting Feedback Gracefully

When people offer you feedback, listen to the information presented, then ask questions to clarify what is meant. Repeat back what they are saying, seeking to understand. Understanding does not mean you agree. That is a different step. Then look at the validity of the info. Accept what is helpful and let the rest go.

Engage in Forgiveness

Everyone has the right to make mistakes. It is a part of being human. Ask for forgiveness, give forgiveness. Act promptly, because waiting just makes it harder. Apologize face to face, showing you understand how you affected them. Ask for forgiveness. If they are open to hearing it, explain what happened. Show how you are going to avoid the problem in the future. Repentance is about changing your behavior. Make restitution where appropriate.

Intentionally Having Fun Together

Building and strengthening your bond as a family happens within shared times together. When we take time to do things together and enjoy each other's company, we are enriching each other's lives. A strong component of a happy life is to have wonderful family relationships that you cherish and nurture. You put time into people you care about who care about you. You build those happy times together sharing meals, fun, and adventures, or working together toward common goals.

In Summary

Family and social connections are strong components of a happy life. We take the time to build and strengthen those connections. We put in boundaries where we need to, but we need to be bonded to other people. We need to take the time and the effort to resolve the disagreements forgive and be forgiven so we can put those disagreements to rest. It enriches our lives to have diverse friends with a wide variety of interests, but still share our core values.

CHAPTER 15

Being Generous to Others

Being Generous with Our Resources

We all have many resources and therefore many opportunities to be generous. Even those who are poor in money and short on time can still find ways to be generous. The purpose of giving is to increase our gratefulness to God for his provision for us and so the storehouses can be full so others can be provided for. When we are generous, it changes our heart toward other people and their needs. Generosity creates in us a sensitivity to the world around us. It moves our focus away from being self-centered and it can add a sense of satisfaction about doing something positive in the world, which adds to our own happiness.

One of the ways to bring value to the world is random acts of kindness. In small or big ways, you can make another person's day go better by intentionally doing something kind. These acts of service and kindness, no matter the size, will make you a happier, more confident person.

Finding Joy in Serving

There are many ways to serve, even those that seem small. Saying a few kind words to a worker in a store. Smiling at people you walk by. Helping someone with a door or a heavy package. Picking up garbage and putting it in a garbage bin. Noticing what people are doing and being appreciative of it. Appreciating the fact that somebody is making your life better by what they are doing and telling them thank you.

When you go into a store, notice that somebody cleans the store, somebody stocks shelves in the store, somebody takes care of the lighting and maintains the aisles so you can easily get what you need. When you see these people, you could take a moment to thank them for what they do.

When you see the delivery person dropping off a package for you, you can say thank you to them. If you know a delivery is coming when you're gone, you could leave a little thank you note for them to make their day happier. It makes somebody smile to know they were appreciated.

Finding regular ways to serve others adds to the richness of your own life while blessing others. Volunteering with disaster relief organizations, helping out with children's programs, helping at homeless missions, cleaning up beaches or roadsides, helping at a library or a community center, there are hundreds of opportunities to serve others and likely dozens of organizations who have volunteer opportunities near you.

Generous with Your Time

Your time is a valuable resource. Every day you have 24 hours, exactly the same amount of time that everyone else in the world has. What you do with your time shows what is important in your life. Giving some of your time to help others, to make the world a better place, is an investment in your own happiness as well.

Being generous with your time does not have to be a big commitment to volunteering. It can include being kind to bus drivers, store clerks, maintenance workers, and servers—all the people you come in contact with during the day. What about being generous with your time when you are driving a vehicle? When you obey the rules of the road, speed limits, distances between vehicles, and the like, you are making the road safer and therefore being kind to all the other people on the road. This is a gift you can easily give others. Similarly, when you wait patiently in a long line, you can be generous with your time and attitude by being kind to those around you, and especially being kind to the person who is serving those in line.

Spending time with young children is another way to be generous with your time. The world is new to a five-year-old and they notice things. They ask questions, and ask questions, and ask questions because they're curious and they wonder about the world. Patiently answering questions is a gift of time to them. That sense of five-year-old curiosity is a blessing, and it brings such joy to your world if you just stop and look at the world around you with them. When we are curious about things with little kids, we don't have time to be sad or depressed and anxious. We can get caught up in their wonder and excitement.

We can serve those in our family by giving time to clean up messes, take out the garbage, scrub down a bathroom, and straighten up a room. When you approach these tasks as a gift you are giving others, it can make the task a joyful act of service rather than a dreaded chore. There is always something you can do to make the world better for those you care about.

Generous with Your Talents

What do you know how to do? You can be generous by sharing your knowledge and skills with others who could benefit from the resources you have. Do you know how to cook, clean, repair a small motor, garden, speak a second language, use a computer, or do a special hobby? You can share that with others while making more social connections.

Ways to Give Back

There are ways to give back to the communities you belong to in more formal ways, too. In a church, you can volunteer to do some of the cleaning, provide some of the children's services, or do some of the office work that's necessary in order for a church to function well. In your community, you could volunteer to pick up garbage along the streets, so the place is in better condition for everybody to live. Where I live, every year there is a beach cleanup day when hundreds of thousands of volunteers come together to pick up the garbage off the beach so we can have clean beaches. There are places that deliver meals to seniors who have a harder time getting out, and there are organizations which list volunteer opportunities. Volunteering is also a good way to make new social connections with other generous people.

Serving Others by Volunteering

Volunteering opens your heart and your world. Helping the poor and the wounded reminds you to see your own growth and how far you have come. Volunteering helps us to be grateful. We get paid richly for volunteering, but not in money. We get paid in the satisfaction of seeing the benefit being made in the world. We get paid in the joy of helping others. We get paid by that feeling of gratefulness for being able to understand the abundance of what we have. As we have mentioned before, contentment is not about the fulfillment of what we want; it's about the realization of how much we already have.

Volunteering gives you the chance to have new, entertaining experiences without cost. You get to learn new things, go new places, meet new people, and have all types of new experiences. All of this fun doesn't cost you money! When the whole family volunteers together, it is a great way for families to bond in a common goal. Children learn to be generous by seeing the model of their parents being generous. Couples volunteering together are building their relationship because they are sharing a purpose.

There are many opportunities to volunteer in your community, with churches, with children's programs, with nonprofit organizations, and with special interest groups. Look around and you can find lots of diverse opportunities.

Generous with Your Money

Being generous is also about giving money. There are a lot of good organizations that are doing good work to help people and make the world a better place. You can join in that work by giving some of your money to them. It takes money to have a building to meet in, to pay the people who organize and run the service projects, and to buy the supplies needed. For a church, it takes money to for the pastor to be able to provide for his family so he can use his time to study and visit the sick and be able to help those who have needs. The reason we give to a church or Christian ministries that help others is so God's storehouse can be full. In that way, others can be helped as these ministries reach out to those in need.

How much money should you give? The amount is not as important as your attitude and that you make it a priority to give money on a regular basis. There is something that changes and grows inside of you as you give. Like any other important skill, it takes effort to learn to be good at it. I suggest you start small and build the muscles you need to do this skill of generosity. The goal is to be able to give cheerfully and gratefully. Maybe start at 1% of your income. Build the attitude and habit. Then you can decide when it is appropriate to raise the amount. Generosity is not just about giving it to the church that you attend, although I think it is a good place to start. Generosity is also about looking around to other places that are also doing good work and giving there as well.

In Summary

We all have many resources and therefore many opportunities to be generous. When we are generous, we increase our gratefulness to God for his provision for us. It changes our heart toward other people and their needs. Generosity can add a sense of satisfaction about doing something positive in the world, which adds to our own happiness. When you serve others through kindness and the generosity of sharing your resources, you will find the ingredients for true joy and satisfaction.

CHAPTER 16

Finding Your Purpose

Knowing how to do the right thing at the right time lowers stress and can increase your happiness and sense of satisfaction. Taking the time to define what your priorities are and in what order are they important to you will help you create a decision-making template when competing agendas show up and people are asking you to do many different things at once. When you know your purpose and what your priorities are, the decisions become easy.

Why do You Get Up in the Morning?

A strong component of happiness is having meaning in what you do every day. Knowing why you get up in the morning. Spending your time engaged in doing meaningful things, things you enjoy, every day. Knowing you are doing the things that need to be done, and doing the things in the order of their importance in your life, gives a feeling of accomplishment and satisfaction. Therefore, finding the purpose of why you get up in the morning makes life happier.

Freedom of Choice

You get to choose your purpose. Your tasks may be placed in front of you, and it may seem like life is laid out for you and you don't feel like you have any choice, but you always have a choice. If every day you get up and go to work making blue widgets and you have to do this job in order to feed your family, it may feel like you have no choice, and yet you do. In that statement, I heard the choice to care for your family, I heard a sense of responsibility and a value of being reliable. Sounds to me like one of your purposes is to provide resources for your family, so they will have what they need. You are prioritizing the gathering of resources for basic needs.

Some people find purpose in serving their family, in making sure that their spouse and their kids have the basic resources that they need. They want to spend time with their family because in that social time they are helping to equip each family member to be able to find and fulfill their passions.

Finding Purpose in Everyday Activities

When you can find the purpose in your daily activities, it makes life happier and easier. When you think beyond the task you are doing, you can find purpose in the task. For example, if you go to a factory every day that makes tires, your job affects your coworkers, your boss, the business, the customers, and other people in the world around you. The single task you do helps tires to be made. The tires sell to customers for a profit so the business can afford to stay open, so people have jobs. The customers use the tires to be able to travel in vehicles. The travel allows the customers to get to work so they can earn resources to provide for their families. Other customers of tires use the vehicles to transport goods and materials to different areas to other people and businesses, so they have the supplies they need to live their lives. Your one task in a tire factory can have a positive effect on thousands of people. So an aspect of your purpose is to bring benefit to the world. When you think beyond yourself, you can experience more happiness.

Priorities and Happiness

Having well-managed priorities helps you to organize your life so you do what is the most important to you. Oftentimes our priorities can get skewed by the urgent rather than the important. If the phone is ringing right now, it seems urgent to answer. But maybe what you are doing right now really needs to be done and it is more important for you to finish your project and let the phone go to voicemail. You can check the voicemail later to see who it was and what they need.

What percentage of the phone calls we get are spam or advertising or marketing? Those are not urgent calls, yet they can disrupt the flow of the important things you are doing. Many other calls from businesses, family, and friends can wait. They do not have to be answered immediately. You can assess your work and home life and decide what level of priority phone calls and emails have in your life. Once you have set the appropriate priority level, the decision about whether to answer now or check messages later becomes clear.

A lot of contacts can wait another hour or two if you are in the middle of doing something that has priority. If you stay focused on your priority of what is important, you can be a lot more productive and get your important tasks accomplished. Then set aside time to check phone calls and messages and deal with those. Many of the other things that seek our attention are not that urgent and generally can wait those few hours to get a response.

Setting Priority Habits

Once I have determined my overall priorities, then it becomes easier to set up habits that will honor those priorities. These are the priorities I see in my life:

- God and Spiritual Life – Without this in order, nothing else works as well.
- Your Self Care – If you do not take care of yourself, you cannot do the rest of the priorities.
- Home and Family – The important grounding of your life.
- Work – By which I bring value to the world and provide resources for myself.

- Business – The business needs to thrive, so I have work.
- Community – A functioning community provides the environment for work and home.

There are times when I will re-evaluate my priorities and see if they fit well in my current situation. But when I have decided what my priorities are, it helps me make day-to-day choices in line with my values. When I do this, I have less stress and more happiness.

Electronic Priorities

One of the ways that I deal with electronic priorities for email, social media, and the phone is that I don't let my phone or computer notify me when I get a message. I will check my messages regularly, but on my schedule, not every moment I get a message. I have decided that level of priority is appropriate for me and the work I do and my family life. Then I have solid blocks of time without being interrupted. Time for electronic media can come in its proper place.

Social Priorities

When time with loved ones is a priority, we find a deep sense of connection and purpose as a part of a larger whole. When people prioritize social interaction, they will almost never work extra hours if it means they have to forego sit-down meals and having a social time with family and friends.

A solid kind of happiness comes from life satisfaction. People don't mind working hard when they live with more purpose and are able to pursue their passions and use their strengths. When people find meaningful ways to engage in life, they are happier. Whether in work or hobbies or creative arts, we like to be engaged in things we like and in which we find purpose.

Social Justice

Some people find purpose in volunteering in their community. They see a need in their community, they take the time to think out how they can help with that need, and they find ways to make life better. They find ways to encourage and equip, to build things up, not tear things down. They get involved in the planning or in the doing of what needs to be done.

Creative Purpose

We are created in the likeness of our creator. That means we are creative. Another way to find purpose is in being able to fulfill your creative desires. When you are someone who is passionate about creating music, art, crafts, writing, online content, organizing, cleaning, gardening, or creating plans that help things to run better, or creating order out of chaos, or enjoying balancing a row of numbers, and an unlimited number of other creative outlets, it gives you a sense of fulfillment and purpose.

In Summary

Managing your purpose and priorities well consists of knowing your purpose and what in your life has the highest priority. Then you arrange your life to honor those priorities so that your happiness is not hindered by life being out of balance.

CHAPTER 17

Spiritual Community

Being connected with a spiritual community is a strong factor in a happy life. We are designed to be deeply connected with others. They add to our happiness, and we add to their happiness. We support and encourage each other. The spiritual community provides a stable base that helps us to heal and grow, to mature, and connect more deeply with our creator. Within this community, we can develop the essential spiritual habits that strengthen connection to God and others, enriching our happiness.

Essential Spiritual Habits

There are many spiritual habits that add to our happiness. Below, I discuss some of them and how they touch our happiness. Each person is a unique individual, and as individuals, we each bring a richness to the spiritual community of which we become a part.

Worship as a Component of Happiness

When we make something more important in our lives than anything else, we are worshiping that thing or individual. Worship of our Lord is a vital part of a Christian's happy life. In worship, we pay a reverent honor to God. Worship is not just singing songs at church services. That is a delightful way to practice a spiritual habit within our social community. Worship is also about every day of our life, all the stuff that we do as a living sacrifice. It's what we do with our minds and how we do our work diligently. It is also when we take a day of rest in worship of God. Individual worship is simply how we spend time with and adore God.

Another part of the worship is when we come together as the body of Christ, as the church, and we worship together. We sing and praise and learn more about God, enjoying each other's company as we declare the greatness of our God.

Prayer

Prayer is an important component of the Christian life and it's essential for our spiritual health. Prayer can be a social community activity where we get together with others and join in a time of prayer together, or a time alone with yourself and God. Prayer is when we are talking to God and listening to God throughout the day. Not just when we want to ask for something but when we acknowledge his presence with us all the time. Prayer changes things. First of all, it changes the person who is praying. When we pray for others, we grow in our awareness of others' needs. We begin to feel more connected to them, concerned for them. Our prayers are a sweet fragrance before God. He listens to us and answers us.

Scripture Study

Another essential habit of a spiritual community is the study of the Scriptures. One of the questions that I like to ask Christians is, "Have you ever read the entire Bible?" I'm surprised at how many Christians have never done that one simple thing. Even if reading it feels like too much, there are many audio Bibles available. You can listen to it for just 10 or 15 minutes a day and listen through the entire Bible in a year. Reading or hearing it all the way through for yourself is one of the ways you are listening for God's words to you.

Bible study is where you go a little deeper. You look at a passage of scripture, pondering what does this actually say. What did it mean to the people who were first reading that passage. The meanings of words in our popular culture change over time, so look up some of the important words in a Bible dictionary, which will give you what the meaning was then.

Then ask yourself "So what?" So what does that mean to my life today? How will I change inside when I let the message of God's word speak to my life and inform my decision and my values? Some people ask, "What does God want for me?" He has given you an entire book to tell you. Have you read it? When we read through the Scriptures, we learn about what God wants for us and expects from us.

Service

Another essential part of spiritual community is a service to one another and service to others who are not part of our community. Service means a number of different things. It could mean you volunteer within the church body that you are attending, helping out in the things that it takes to run the ministries of the church. Service could mean you look around in your community where you can help others. Serve where you could make the world a little better place by the things that you do.

Relationships in Spiritual Community

We are created to be in the community. The Christian life is not designed to be alone, just between us and God. Scripture tells us that we are all part of one body. The hands can't tell the feet that they don't need them, the eye can't tell the ears it doesn't need them. In the same way, we can't say to other Christians, "We don't need you." Sometimes it you hear people say, "Well you know I'm fine this week. I don't need to go to church because I don't need anything. I'm doing fine." Are you aware that they need you? Meeting together is not just to fill you up. It is also about what you bring to them. Supporting and encouraging each other is a two-way thing. It is your relationship with them *and* their relationship with you.

Sharing Your Lives

Growing together, sharing your lives with each other, is another part of the Christian life. In this way, you share a witness of how God is at work in your life. We are not all called to preach, but we are all called to be a witness. A witness just tells what they have seen, what they have heard, and what they know. It is about living life out loud, integrating your faith into your life. When somebody asks you how your weekend was, do you include telling them about the wonderful song at church that you really enjoyed? And about what you heard in the message or in a Bible study? Sharing your faith can also be having a ready answer for questions you're asked when people see the hope that is within you. When they ask about the joy that they see in you, the strength they see in you as you go through struggles and trials, do you tell them the hope you find in God?

In Summary

Being connected with a spiritual community is a strong factor in a happy life. We are designed to be deeply connected with others. Each person is a unique individual, and as individuals we each bring a richness to the spiritual community of which we become a part.

Within the community we develop spiritual habits that strengthen our connection to God and others, enriching our happiness.

CHAPTER 18

Abundant Life – Putting It All Together

In this book, we explored three areas of abundant life. To have abundance refers to having more than an adequate supply, to have plenty or more than you need. Abundance is the opposite of scarcity. We learned how we can live in abundance, having confidence, contentment, and happiness. Learning these skills of healthy behavior will bring joy and happiness.

We looked at the freedoms and joys of responsible adulthood, the skills adults use to live an abundant life, creating confidence, learning contentment, and creating happiness for themselves and others. You can have the freedom of recognizing and enjoying the richness of life around you, whether you have little or much. You can leave behind the crippling mindset of scarcity and its struggles, developing the mature habits of an abundance mentality, healthy relationships, a heart at peace, and the diligent choices that move toward looking at your future with confidence.

There is a workbook that accompanies each of the four books in this Trauma Healing Series. The workbooks will help you with practical exercises of how you can develop the insight and skills to put all this healing together in an abundant way.

Confidence

Confidence gives a sense of power and freedom to your life. Having confidence is the feeling or belief that you can do something well; a calm reliance on yourself, someone else or something. Self-confidence is a skill you can build and strengthen. It is knowing when you are doing the right things at the right times, in the right ways, for the right reasons.

A person with confidence is at ease with themselves and generally very easy to be around. They get along well with most people in most situations. They have a sense of direction and self-assurance. They show that they have strong values by the respectful way they treat others and expect to be treated themselves. Since they feel at ease within themselves, the people they are around can feel at ease as well.

Confident adults interact with others on a basis of equality. There are times and places in life where we need to ask for permission because we don't have the authority to do something. But there are other times and places that we have the authority to decide what we will do, and we don't need to ask anybody else's permission because as an adult we have that authority to make decisions in our own lives.

When we take the time to develop skills and competence, it is easy to feel confident. Competence grows as our talents and strengths are recognized and built up. We have a sense that we are good at trying. Even when life gets stressful, we figure out how to cope. We work through difficult problems and mistakes, expanding our knowledge and skill along the way; our accomplishments are the result of a combination of ability, effort, study, training, practice, and experience. When we have competence, we have the skills and ability to do something successfully.

A major part of the skill-building of confidence is knowing what is essential to you. What are the values that you hold dear? Values are what we have determined are important to us, the principles that help you decide what is useful, good, right, and desirable. Values have a major influence on a person's behaviors and attitudes and serve as broad guidelines in choosing what actions are best to do or what way is best to live.

Making confident decisions is when you know you are doing the right things for the right reasons. An important aspect of values is the way our decisions are made in regard to all our resources. When you sort out your values and what your priorities are, it gives you the confidence to be able to say no when you need to say no and to say yes where you need to say yes. Your confidence comes from time spent working out your decision-making matrix. When I make decisions in line with my values, then I can have confidence that I've made the right decision, even if it is not a comfortable or easy decision. After I've sorted out my priorities, I can make the decisions that I make and look at them in line with my priorities. I then have confidence in what I should do because I know what's important to me.

One of the most significant ways to build your confidence is by understanding the "why" of your life and everything you do. When you take a new job, make a big decision, or start a new project, ask yourself why you are doing this. What is the bigger reason behind your actions? Knowing your "why" gives you the confidence that your judgment is solid. When I am evaluating my own choices, it is good to look deeply into not only what did I do, but what did I want, and what led to this outcome? Then I can confidently look at the strength of my choices or the things I actually need to change.

Contentment

When you have contentment, you are at ease with yourself and your life. You know how to ask for what you want, and how to make decisions that respect your values and the values of others. You are aware of your influence in the world. There is a deep freedom in contentment, a sense of knowing your place in the world. Contentment is an attitude of heart that you can develop. Contentment is not the fulfillment of what you want but rather the realization of what you already have.

So asking for what I want means I need to be aware of how what I'm asking for is going to affect my life and the lives of others around me. Asking for what I want is not a demand I'm making, but a request for something I would like to have. I'm open to whatever the answer is going to be. If the answer is yes, that's great. If the answer is no, I will accept that. Having contentment is learning to be able to be content whether you have much or little

Each of us has a lot of resources. We can be content with our resources, or we can be dissatisfied and always striving for what we don't yet have. Your resources are those assets you can draw on in order to fulfill a purpose or need or to function effectively, something from which a benefit is produced that enhances the quality of your life. Resources are a means of accomplishing something or a source of strength or ability within yourself.

To be content with resources is about learning to recognize the resources you have, valuing them for the benefit they can bring to your life and the lives of others. Know all material resources are temporary. When people focus on money as the most valuable resource, it plunges them into a discontented life that does not end well. In their drive to get rich, they can lose sight of more important resources like integrity, family, health, and time.

When you have contentment, you are at ease with yourself and your life and at ease with those around you. When we feel contentment, we accept people for who they are and don't spend our time trying to get them to change to how we want them to be. Therefore, a lot of conflict goes away. People are different than you. They have different ways of seeing the world and different opinions about what is important. In those very differences is a wider and richer view of the world. Contentment in social relationships means we respect their right to be different, and we treat them with respect.

We can effect change in the world around us through the ways we affect others: influence, modeling, parenting, authority, and position. We get to choose whether that is for good or ill. All of us influence other people not just with our words but more so with our behavior.

When you have contentment, you are at ease with yourself and your life. There is a deep freedom in contentment. But freedom without responsibility can become just an excuse for selfish distain for other people's freedom. There are limits to our freedom.

Being responsible means that people can count on you to do the next right thing. They can count on you being where you said you would be when you said you would be there. Other people never have to wonder or worry about where you are and what you are doing. Responsible people choose to be accountable for their own actions. Responsible people take care of their own tasks and help out other people.

A lot of life is out of our control. Maybe most of it. Acceptance means we understand this truth. We are affected by circumstances we did not create; we have to go through pain and discomfort we cannot change. But we do not have to be trapped in misery. We suffer in misery when we fight against the facts that we cannot change. Acceptance of those facts does not mean that we agree with them, nor does it mean that we are helpless victims of them. We simply accept this is what is and now what is our response going to be. Pain is inevitable; misery is optional.

You are the one who chooses your level of contentment in life.

Happiness

An attitude of abundance does not rely on how much you have. It is a state of mind, as is happiness. Happiness is an enjoyable or satisfying feeling when life is pleasurable. It ranges from mild enjoyment to an intense delight. Components of happiness include caring for your own physical, emotional, and mental needs; connections to family and a social community; bringing value to the world; having well-thought-out priorities; and cultivating a spiritual life, including connecting in a faith-based community. You can create a richness of life that goes far beyond the temporary rewards of success and create a lasting happiness for yourself in any situation and to bring more happiness into the life of others.

It is important to care for your own needs, but not only your own needs. However, before you will have resources to care for others—another vital component of happiness—you need to function well in the basic self-care skills of adulthood.

Our family and social connections are a vital component in our happiness. Family can consist of all the people who support and love us, the people we can confide in and trust. Family means having someone to love you unconditionally in spite of you and your shortcomings. Family is loving and supporting one another even when it's not easy to do so.

People in a family have respect and appreciation of each other no matter how old, how young, where each one comes from, what they have experienced, where they are, how capable they are, how healthy they are, or who they love. Family is always there in good times and not so good times. Family includes all the people in our lives who commit to love and support us unconditionally. It is not a passive birthright, but a choice we make of love, commitment, and kindness that helps us thrive both as individuals and as a family. Even when things go wrong, you can always depend on family. Family brings you back to your values and helps you make good decisions.

We all have many resources and therefore many opportunities to be generous. The purpose of giving is to increase our gratefulness to God for his provision for us. Another purpose of giving is so the storehouses can be full so others can be provided for. When we are generous, it changes our heart toward other people and their needs. Generosity creates in us a sensitivity to the world around us, moving our focus away from being self-centered. It can add a sense of satisfaction about doing something positive in the world, which adds to our own happiness.

One of the ways to bring value to the world is random acts of kindness. In small ways or big things, you can make another person's day go better by intentionally doing something kind. These acts of service and kindness can be big or small, but they will make you a happier, more confident person.

A strong component of happiness is having meaning in what you do every day and knowing why you get up in the morning. Spending your time engaged in doing meaningful things, things that you enjoy, every day leads to a greater sense of happiness. Knowing that you are doing the things that need to be done gives a feeling of accomplishment and satisfaction, especially if they are done in the order of their importance, with regard to their priority level in your life. Finding the purpose of why you get up in the morning makes life happier.

Being connected with a spiritual community is a strong factor in a happy life. We are designed to be deeply connected with others. They add to our happiness, and we add to their happiness. We support, and encourage each other. A spiritual community provides a stable base that helps us to heal and grow, to mature and connect more deeply with our creator. Within this community, we can develop the essential spiritual habits that strengthen our connection to God and others, enriching our happiness. The habits of prayer, meditation, fellowship, generosity, kindness and others help us to grow into a richer happiness.

In Summary

This is the fourth book in the Trauma Healing Series, exploring the differences between a healthy, functional life and a wounded life impacted by the lingering effects of bullying, abuse, trauma, neglect, domestic violence, substance use, and chaos. This series is designed to help lower the barriers that hinder growth and healing so you can move forward toward the freedom of thriving.

In book one, *Fundamentals*, the basic rights of a human were explored, along with how to escape the lingering effects of bullying, abuse, or trauma. It teaches you how to develop an inner awareness of your strengths and understand the contrast to past chaos, so you can step into freedom, abundance, security, and significance, and be happy. *Fundamentals* explores how to have more peace within yourself, better relationships with others, and more freedom and contentment, no matter what is going on around you.

Book two, *Restoration*, discussed how we are designed to live in joy and peace and be able to heal from the wounds of life. We looked deeply into our unique design. We saw that we could put to rest the old wounds that trap us into painful patterns of responding to life and hinder healing, strengthening healthy patterns of living. We can live our best life after trauma.

In book three, *Connections*, we looked at mastering the art of relationships. When you do what it takes to develop wholesome social habits and essential boundary skills, you can have good relationships now and in the future, no matter what your past relationships were like. By learning key skills for a healthy lifestyle and safe, healthy relationships, you unlock the power of community to discover your significant place in the world.

Finally, in this fourth book, you have read about having the confident freedom of contentment, recognizing and enjoying the abundance of life around you. By using the principles in this book, you will derive a richness of life that goes far beyond the temporary rewards of success and create lasting happiness for yourself in any situation.

Contentment is not the fulfillment of what you want, but the realization of what you already have.

There are a set of workbooks that is part of the series. The four workbooks help with additional exercises and thoughts to help you move deeper into your healing and growth journey.

Afterword

Faith's Story of Abundance

In my earliest years, I experienced scarcity. There were times when my most basic needs seemed hard to get. Decades of my life were spent living with trauma. I grew up in the midst of extreme poverty, occasional homelessness, and all kinds of abuse. I never thought of us as poor. I just thought that this was what life was. We moved a lot when I was a child. In the rush to move, and the lack of space to pack things, a little girl's stuff was treated with no importance. I learned not to get attached to stuff, because I would not have it long. I would enjoy it while I had it but trusted no future with it.

Life lessons in those early years taught me the importance of contentment. It taught me that vital resources were scarce. The safe nurturing I needed as a child was especially scarce. The wounds of an abused child linger into adulthood in a number of ways. Having a scarcity mentality was one of the ways it lingered in my life. I did not look for friends because I thought safe, nurturing friends were scarce. I did not trust people to be kind because I had experienced a scarcity of kindness. Adulthood seemed to be a dangerous place where one had to constantly be on guard against destructive forces.

When I healed from the past traumas, I looked around and saw a different world. Because of the healing inside of me, I was now able to recognize how much kindness, friendliness, and richness was around me. I was looking through an abundance mentality and saw resources available everywhere, lots of kind people, and contentment. It reminded me of what I knew from my earliest thoughts.

God loves me whether I am in a scarcity mentality or an abundance mentality. God is more concerned with my character development than my comfort. I have a tendency to be more concerned with my comfort. I like to be comfortable, but it is during the uncomfortable times that my character can develop. Now I see that although life is hard, often disappointing, and painful, misery does not get to trap me in its suffering. God provides an abundance within me even when life is hard. It comes through Jesus.

Jesus is the way. John 3:16 states that "God so loved the world that he sent his only son that whosoever believes in him should not perish but have eternal life." I find that such a wonderfully comforting statement. The "whosoever" means this offer is open to me. It's open to anybody and everybody. No one is too bad or too wrong or too different. God made all of us. The offer is something we have to accept in order to have the eternal life he offers. When we accept Jesus as Savior and Lord, we are agreeing with God that we have done wrong. Confessing to him what we have done and accepting him into our life as Lord and Savior gives us salvation. The Lord part means that then I want to obey him. He is not going to make me obey him, but because I love him and because he loves me, I want to obey. So, I spend time reading his Word. I spend time with his people, so I am connected and growing more like him.

This invitation to abundant life is open to anyone and everyone. Not everyone chooses to accept Jesus as Lord and Savior, but that is who he is in my life. He is my savior, my lord, my friend, and my guide to a healthy life.

Other books by Faith Winters

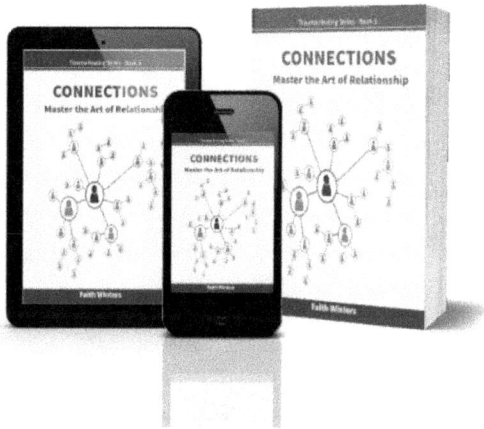

www.ingramcontent.com/pod-product-compliance
Lightning Source LLC
Chambersburg PA
CBHW060246050426
42448CB00009B/1585